MATRIX
ENERGETICS

MATRIX ENERGETICS

THE SCIENCE AND ART OF TRANSFORMATION

Richard Bartlett, DC, ND

Foreword by William A. Tiller, PhD

ATRIA PAPERBACK
New York London Toronto Sydney

BEYOND WORDS
Hillsboro, Oregon

ATRIA PAPERBACK
A Division of Simon & Schuster, Inc.
1230 Avenue of the Americas
New York, NY 10020

BEYOND WORDS
20827 NW Cornell Road, Suite 500
Hillsboro, Oregon 97124-9808
503-531-8700 / 503-531-8773 fax
www.beyondword.com

Editors: Hal Zina Bennett and Julie Knowles
Managing editor: Henry Covi, Lindsay S. Brown
Copyediting/proofreading: Meadowlark Communications, Inc.
Cover and interior design: Carol Sibley, Devon Smith
Composition: William H. Brunson Typography Services

First Atria Paperback / Beyond Words trade paperback edition July 2009

ATRIA PAPERBACK and colophon are trademarks of Simon & Schuster, Inc.
Beyond Words Publishing is a division of Simon & Schuster, Inc.

For more information about special discounts for bulk purchases, please contact Simon & Schuster Special Sales at 1-866-506-1949 or business@simonandschuster.com.

The Simon & Schuster Speakers Bureau can bring authors to your live event.
For more information or to book an event contact the Simon & Schuster Speakers Bureau at 1-866-248-3049 or visit our website at www.simonspeakers.com.

Manufactured in the United States of America

10 9 8 7 6 5 4 3 2 1

The Library of Congress has cataloged the hardcover edition as follows:

Bartlett, Richard.
    Matrix energetics : the science and art of transformation / by Richard Bartlett.—1st Atria Books/Beyond Words hardcover ed.
        p. cm.
    Includes bibliographical references.
    1. Energy—Therapeutic use. 2. Vital force—Therapeutic use. I. Title.
RZ421.B37 2007
615.5'3—dc22
                                                                        2006029675

ISBN: 978-1-58270-163-9 (hc)
ISBN: 978-1-58270-238-4 (pbk)

The corporate mission of Beyond Words Publishing, Inc.: *Inspire to Integrity*

*This book and probably myself would not exist without the constant,
loving, capable, ever-vigilant and patient dedication
of my wife, Cynthia Bartlett.
To her I owe the deepest gratitude and dedicate this book.*

PUBLISHER'S NOTE

Unlimited thinking has been a fundamental value behind the editorial vision at Beyond Words since we began publishing books. Few original ideas and ways of thinking would emerge from old paradigms without the unpredictable potential of our minds. The methods and techniques taught by Dr. Richard Bartlett in *Matrix Energetics*, along with the supporting theories of Dr. William A. Tiller in the foreword, represent an inspiring fusion of unrestricted thinking by encompassing the realms of art and science—and in so doing fusing imagination with the practical laws of manifestation. Thank you for reading, and enjoy *Matrix*!

—Cynthia Black, editor in chief

CONTENTS

FOREWORD

THIS IS A TERRIFIC, REMARKABLE, TRANSFORMATIVE BOOK. I have enjoyed experiencing it. It could also have been titled *The Way of a Modern-Day Shaman* or *Structural Alchemy for Transforming Humans* without any loss of authenticity.

Dr. Richard Bartlett is truly a man of miracles. In *Matrix Energetics*, he has grasped and owned an essential operating principle of nature: that we are all co-creators of our personal reality whether we consciously choose to be or not. Life, in the higher-dimensional and subtler domains of our overall reality, has worked hard to keep Dr. Bartlett both alive and astonishingly capable, and has blessed him with manifested gifts of a high order. It is as though he was meant to be here in this earth-plane society at this time to materialize these gifts of human transformation and to teach others that they can do likewise.

Early on, Dr. Bartlett paints a clear picture of the difficulty that exists for people who go from doctor to doctor trying to cure their uncertain health problems via self-diagnosis based on their symptoms. The psycho-physiological principle, which always operates in the client, blurs the edges of all the symptoms so that, more often than not, one ends up with a completely mixed "symptom soup" that cannot be unmixed.

Dr. Bartlett avoids the common way of thinking that treats clients as well-specified problem-sets that have well-specified solution-sets. Rather, he adopts the quantum mechanics metaphor that there is a virtual sea of possible solutions; there, you are free to use your imagination and pick one that you like. He recognizes that even when a metaphor is not factually correct as stated, the concept you visualize can have significant power to drive an action from an entirely different level of reality than you anticipate, bringing about a structural change in the physical body so that it now appears to work properly, sometimes for the first time.

The term "Matrix Energetics" comes from books on energy medicine by James Oschman, who in turn was inspired by the work of Alfred Pischinger, author of *Matrix and Matrix Regulation: Basis for a Holistic Theory in Medicine*. In both Pischinger and Oschman's work, the term deals only with our normal, electric atom/molecule level of physical reality. Dr. Bartlett, on the other hand, thinks that we are basically constructed from light and information and are thus malleable to focused intent. Under this rubric, Matrix Energetics is an archetype; practioners maintain a state of awareness and enter into a kind of energetic rapport with clients, holding for them what shamanic cultures call "sacred space" so that they can have the freedom to express a different outcome for their physical states.

There are many emerging scientific details involved in Matrix Energetics, but it isn't necessary to know the underlying facts as long as the intended change is visualized clearly, the belief is strong, and the emotional force behind the intention is both focused and sustained.

In the interest of expanding the reader's understanding of this important field of future science, I would like to provide a picture of the way I see Matrix Energetics working.

As figure 1 indicates, we can think of *every* human interaction as occurring via five uniquely distinguishable parts. Key components here are the "Electromagnetic Gauge-Symmetry State," within which the interaction-event is taking place, and the "Unseen Universe." Anyone who has had firsthand experience with Dr. Bartlett knows that the unseen works strongly through him into this world.

My research on psychoenergetic science, as well as that of my colleagues, has revealed the existence of a *second*, unique level of physical reality that may or may not be strongly coupled with our normal par-

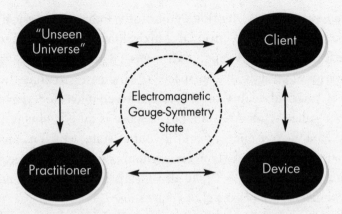

Figure 1
Every one of us can influence all biological life forms around us via our biofield emissions and the information that they carry, whether we intend to or not.

ticulate electric atom/molecule level of physical reality, that which we are all cognitively aware of at the conscious level. At present, only our unconscious is aware of this new magnetic information wave level of physical reality that functions at superluminal velocities in the physical vacuum-level space between the fundamental electric particles that comprise our atoms and molecules. Properties of physical materials, inanimate or animate, can be approximately described by the simple equation:

$$Q(t) = Q_e(t) + \alpha_{eff}(t) Q_m(t)$$

Here, $Q(t)$ is the total magnitude of the material property under consideration; $Q_e(t)$ is the contribution from the electric atom/molecule level; $Q_m(t)$ is the contribution from the magnetic information wave level; α_{eff} is the effective coupling coefficient between these two levels of substance; and t is time.

Our research has shown that, when α_{eff} is negligible, as is the case in our normal world state, our traditional physics of materials applies. Then, the second term in the equation essentially disappears and human intention cannot significantly influence physical reality because only our conventional Maxwellian equations of electromagnetic (EM) reality apply. However, with a sufficient field of consciousness present in the space, α_{eff} increases so that these two levels of physical reality are significantly coupled and the electromagnetic gauge symmetry state of the space is raised. This is a higher thermodynamic free energy per unit volume state, which means that it can do useful work of any type on a system of lower-EM gauge symmetry state (one with $\alpha_{eff} \approx 0$). It also means that *human intention can strongly influence the physics of this duplex space.*

Our research has also indicated that the human acupuncture meridian/ chakra system exists at this higher-EM gauge symmetry state, so that focused and sustained human intention channeled through this system can produce amazing transformation both inside and outside the body.

The next piece of the picture we need in order to understand how Matrix Energetics works is my working hypothesis concerning what constitutes a whole person. This is illustrated in figure 2 and should be visualized as a three-zone sphere-like construct. The outermost zone consists of the two-layered physical bio bodysuit that we put on when we are born into this space-time reality of experience and shuck off when we die, passing from this domain of experience. I label this our "Personality Self" with the outermost layer being made of particulate, electric atom/molecule stuff and the inner layer being made of our magnetic, information-wave stuff.

The middle zone is our "Soul Self," constructed from emotion domain substance, mind domain substance, and indwelling spirit domain substance, which is the major self that is evolving here. The substance that constitutes α_{eff} in the equation is presently thought to come from the emotion domain level.

The central zone in this construct is called the "High Self, the "God Self," or the "Source Self."

Figure 2
My metaphor for the whole person.

Just as the outermost layer of the Personality Self involves at least the four accepted and fundamental forces (gravity, electromagnetism, the long-range—"strong"—nuclear force, and the short-range—"weak"—nuclear force), each of the other unique layers probably involve just as many uniquely different energies that we have not yet discovered. Thus, the interplay of many, many different kinds of energy is involved in the lawful functioning of living systems. Each of these different types of energy can be thought of as a single term in a large mathematical matrix representation of such a living system. Matrix Energetics, as a name, is a useful metaphor for such a system—anything you can imagine can ultimately be created in this 10-dimensional simulator, which is illustrated by the schematic representation in figure 3.

Human intention is thought to be created in the domain of spirit (the 11-dimensions and above construct) and appears in the simulator

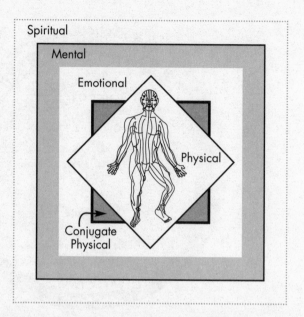

Figure 3
A representation of our reference frame (RF) with the duplex space in the center. If one counts the entire duplex space as a 4-space, then the entire multidimensional representation is a 7-space. If instead, we count the duplex space as a unique member of the general 8-space, then our reference frame is 11-dimensional.

as a specific pattern of information at the mind level of this simulator. This information pattern is then radiated from the mind nodal network to activate the emotion domain quality that increases the α_{eff} in the equation and imprints a conjugate pattern of information on the magnetic information wave domain (the conjugate physical space in figure 3). This in turn adjusts the quality of Q_m in the equation to be in accord with the original intention. This is how the simulator is ideally thought to create anything one intends from the domain of spirit in space-time (the physical space in figure 3).

Returning to figure 1, all five magnetic information wave contributions are vectors, so that in the ultimate outcome effect that manifests via the equation, each vector's information entangles with each other, in pairs. Thus, for example, the degree of tuning of the practitioner to the client can change the magnitude of this practitioner/client term from a zero value to a maximum-plus value to a minimum-minus value just by shifting from being completely in-phase with the other person.

Of course, to complicate things, one must also consider the tunings between each of the three parts of the whole person selves illustrated in figure 2.

The bottom line in all this is that what appears to be pure magic in Dr. Bartlett's healing treatments is, in fact, a rational manipulation of energies and information in a lawful fashion based upon his theoretical construct of reality, which is appreciably "outside the box" of our present paradigm. Even without such a theoretical model, Dr. Bartlett is such a well-qualified channel for the unseen to work through into this world that together, he and his clients produce the necessary fields of energy in the different dimensions of our overall reality, and harmony and balance are restored to the client. And what he and the client can do, so can others.

As a species, we are cognitively moving away from space-time awareness only and into frequency domain (conjugate physical-space) awareness. In the latter domain, distance and time are not limitations to our perceptions. You can see this at work in *Matrix Energetics*. I recommend this book as important reading for everyone!

—William A. Tiller, PhD,
Professor Emeritus, Stanford University

PREFACE

Each new generation of our human community has been inspired by the science of its time. Principles that we may or may not fully understand, but that we intuitively know to be true, reshape our thinking, and in doing so, reshape our experience of the world and what we may be willing to do. During Galileo's time, the idea that the sun, not the earth, was the center of the universe nearly cost him his head. As it was, it silenced him and forced him into obscurity for the rest of his life. Nevertheless, his discoveries changed the way we all think about the world and our relationship to it. Such discoveries change us whether we know science or not. In many cases, those changes are quite dramatic.

The scientific icons that influence us today are no less revolutionary than they were in Galileo's time. In fact, they may be even more revolutionary because they change our way of looking at and working with the physical world. At the heart of today's physics are ideas that stimulate and inspire our imaginations in ways that are nothing short of startling. Most of us do not have a sufficient grasp of higher mathematics to explain these new ideas as a physicist might, but this does not diminish the impact of science on our creative consciousness.

The key concepts of quantum physics teach us that we are one with our universe and that we are inextricably connected together by a mysterious energy called the Zero Point Energy Field. Zero Point Energy is the sea of virtual particles that lies beneath every point in the universe. If we were to cool these particles as close as we possibly could to absolute zero, there should be, according to the postulates of Newtonian science, no energy there. Instead, much to the astonishment of scientists, there still remains an immense quantity of energy at this Zero Point. Some scientists have actually called this energy the Mind of God. This sounds a lot like the mystical "Force" of George Lucas's *Star Wars* to me. Renowned physicist John Wheeler has called this energy "a meaning software, located who-knows-where." Such ideas and discoveries have profoundly altered our concepts about who we humans are and our importance in the grand scheme of things.

Quantum physics is not something I would have chosen to study intensely, but Life has a way of changing your course and shaking up all of your cherished assumptions. I was in my first semester of Chiropractic school when my wife gave birth to a child who, for the next several years, would be plagued by many health challenges, and who would become my personal teacher and Muse in my quest to find something, *anything*, that could heal him. He was born with a seriously compromised immune system. During the first three years of his life, he was saddled with a body that had chronic bronchitis and developed pneumonia every six weeks.

When conventional medical wisdom and alternative healing methods failed to help him, I resolved to take on the challenge myself. Realizing that I was not finding any answers in my medical training, I embarked on a journey to learn whatever the medical institutions were not teaching. Making the school library my home base, I hungrily devoured all of the eclectic—what some would call "weird"—healing wisdom that I could find. This search for answers left me with a lifelong habit of asking unusual questions and then following wherever the information led me. In his third year of life, something I learned instantly healed my son. This event set the course of my strange and wonderful journey into mystical and magical realms: a kind of Hogwarts school of wizardry and healing. I took the road less traveled and have never once looked back.

In 1996, while I was attending Naturopathic medical school, another event radically altered the entire course of my existence. You will read about what happened in the first chapter, so I won't put any plot spoilers in this preface. My life has not been the same since that event, and after reading this book, I am betting that yours never will be either!

Changes occurred in me that were so radical in their scope that I am still reeling from their effects and ramifications years later. When I began to teach what I now could do, I needed a common language that would make Matrix Energetics easily teachable to anyone. The magical and perplexing world of quantum physics turned out to contain the keys to that language.

When I started applying the principles of quantum science, everything fell into place. I seized on the idea that at the bedrock of our physical reality we are made up of high-energy photons, the smallest known particles of matter. We are, in our essence, just patterns of light and information. When you truly grasp this concept, it unlocks the power to interact with the Zero Point Energy Field, to draw on the power of "the force." When you begin to see everything in this manner, it can profoundly change every aspect of your life. You are not separate from any other part of life, but are linked with that indivisible One spirit.

I am neither a mathematician nor a physicist, but I have been profoundly influenced by the contributions of quantum physics. The knowledge I have of these principles could be described as more "poetic" and "imaginative" than scientific, and I heartily agree with such characterizations. Like those living in the post-Galileo world who had to shift their perspective of their relationship to the heavenly bodies, I and those around me, including my students, have made shifts that have been deeply influenced by quantum principles.

I have now taught Matrix Energetics to thousands of people in every walk of life, and it works. The ideas underlying Matrix Energetics unlock the power that resides within us all to transform our existence in every imaginable way, and now they are available to those of you reading this book. These ideas and tools I offer are not meant just for healers; they are for everyone who wants to transform their experience into something unique and powerful. Matrix Energetics represents an entirely new paradigm; its principles can literally transform how you see and experience your world. But don't take my word for it. Read what one of my students was able to do for herself after taking only one life-changing weekend seminar—and then decide for yourself.

I was reading in *Science News* about the Bose-Einstein condensate process for freezing gas, which could then be bombarded with lasers, making equal amounts of both hot and cold particles at the same time. This gave me an idea. I have had a palpable uterine fibroid for some time, so I used one of the Matrix Energetics techniques and "Two-Pointed" my uterus. As I did this I was thinking, "What would it be like if the tumor was a condensate, and lasers vaporized the composition of its particles so they were hot and cold at the same time?"

That night I felt the fibroid and it was half its previous size. Two nights later it was gone. I am one who believes this Matrix Energetics stuff is great, and now I believe it works with me. Seeing it work with others is one part of knowing it works, and having it be successful with myself as the subject is phenomenal. What a great shift in my reality. My best to you, and thanks again.

—Kathleen Martin, Santa Barbara

ACKNOWLEDGMENTS

I WISH TO THANK Dr. Jacques L. Rowe, DC, my first mentor, who showed me that you could see beyond the veil and that energy medicine was real and powerful.

I also deeply and humbly thank Dr. Victor Frank, DC, developer of the TBM Healing System, whose gift of knowledge allowed me to heal my son of bronchitis, asthma, and pneumonia and who has been like a father.

I wish to thank Dr. M. L. Rees, DC, who taught me how to merge technology and magic. A "True Wizard," he is deeply missed.

I wish to thank my teacher, Dr. Richard Bandler, developer of Neuro-Linguistic Programming (NLP). I've read many books by various authors that are heavily influenced by NLP and very rarely is credit given to Dr. Bandler. I wish to give credit where credit is due.

Thanks to my friend and mentor Dr. David Denton, DC, who taught me the wonders of healing through manipulation of the human cranium.

I wish to pay deep, humble gratitude to my spiritual teacher, Elizabeth Claire Prophet, who taught me it is okay "not to know" and that spirituality is practicality, and who deeply loved me with all my flaws.

I wish to thank my friend Betsy Bergstom, who introduced me to shamanic states of consciousness and showed me the validity and power of that realm.

On the scientific side of things I wish to acknowledge and thank my friend Dr. Karl Pribram, developer of the concept of the nervous system as a holographic phenomenon, and my dear friend, Dr. William Tiller, who encouraged and revolutionized my thinking concerning scientific concepts and how they can be applied in a magical dimension of possibilities.

I must thank and apologize for tormenting my editors Regi Shelley, Hal Zina Bennett, and Julie Knowles.

Thanks to Cynthia Black, owner of Beyond Words Publishing, who caught the vision, felt the magic, and insisted that she publish my book.

I want to thank all my students throughout the world, especially my first student Mark Filippi, Master Wizard and dear friend, and all my master teachers and facilitators without whom I could not teach my seminars.

I want to thank my children Justice, Nathaniel, Victor, and Dara for teaching and healing me, and my dog Xena, goddess of freaky events.

Finally, I give heartfelt thanks to my dear friend, Dr. Mark Dunn, ND, who saw what I could do, wanted what I have, and refused to leave until he made that reality his own. He paved the way for everyone after him and made it possible for Matrix Energetics to exist as a seminar and in this book. He is an amazing, tireless, dedicated, wonderful friend and I will always hold him in the highest regard.

PART 1

The Birth of Matrix Energetics

THE LITTLE GIRL WAS THREE YEARS OLD. She arrived with her mother at my chiropractic office at 6 PM, the last patient of a very exhausting day. I had driven four hours to get to my office in Livingston, Montana, that morning. The night before, I had stopped to sleep at a motel in Missoula, Montana, too exhausted to complete the drive from Seattle. I was enrolled in Bastyr Naturopathic University, taking a course load of thirty-one credits a semester in order to earn my degree in Naturopathy. Even with my heavy academic schedule, I still had to put food on the table for my family. I had not yet passed the Washington State Chiropractic board exam, which necessitated the bimonthly trek to Montana where my chiropractic practice was still flourishing, in spite of my very part-time schedule there.

Notwithstanding the title of "chiropractor," I had somewhat of a reputation in my local community for being this strange guy who practiced weird medicine. I was accustomed to unusual cases arriving at my doorstep. In this instance, the mother told me that her little girl had gone to the neurologist and had been diagnosed with a lazy eye. The doctor told her that there wasn't any treatment or surgery that he would recommend. If she wore an eye patch, maybe she would outgrow it by the time she was a teenager. The mother looked at me and said, "Well, that's not good enough for me. What do you think?"

I went into a deep trance, no doubt induced by sleep deprivation, and started babbling about a television episode of *Superman* that I saw in the 1950s. In this particular show, a little blind girl wins an essay contest sponsored by the *Daily Planet*. The prize is a trip around the world with Superman. When Clark, Lois, and Jimmy go to her New York apartment to meet her, Clark is stunned to find out that she's blind. Perplexed by this strange turn of events he asks, "Sweetheart, why would you want to fly around the world with Superman?" The child replies matter-of-factly, "Superman doesn't really exist, but I want the *Daily Planet* to fly Mommy around the world so she can find my Daddy."

In this episode, the girl's father Dan had been out for a nice weekend drive with his young family and had a terrible accident while swerving to avoid a pedestrian. The family car had run headlong into a corner lamp post, shattering the car's windshield and showering the occupants with shards of broken glass.

It was not immediately apparent after the accident that their young daughter could not see. She was an infant, so it was difficult to tell at first. The specialist they took her to confirmed the awful truth; she was totally blind. When asked what their options were, the doctor replied sadly that there was nothing he could do. In an effort to comfort the distraught parents, the doctor wistfully explained that sometimes blindness just goes away after a spell, but that they should not get their hopes up too high.

The family struggled to stay together in spite of the terrible stress and guilt the father had been experiencing ever since the incident. After many months of living with a crippling case of guilt, the man could bear it no longer. Every time he looked into his wife's eyes he saw accusation in her gaze. Unable to look at his daughter any longer, he left one night and never returned home. A friend, when queried, reported hearing Dan say that he was going to join the Foreign Legion or something.

Saddened to tears by this tragic story, Clark decides that there must be something he can do. What good is it to have super powers if you just have to stand by helplessly? He realizes that if he is going to do anything in this situation, he must start by convincing the little girl that he is indeed Superman. Spying an iron poker leaning against the fireplace, he walks over and brings it back to where she is quietly sitting. With gentle resolve he holds the iron implement out for her to feel, then gently places the rod behind her, and bends it slowly into a ring that encompasses her frail neck. Stunned, she whispers, "You *really are* Superman. No one else could do that!"

With a sad smile Superman replies, "Yes, I am, honey," and kneels down to gently reshape the steel poker into its original form.

As he kneels in front of her he notices with his X-ray vision that there is a little piece of glass in her eye, lodged near the optic nerve; perhaps that could be the cause of her blindness. Later that day Superman talks to a surgeon, who agrees to perform exploratory surgery (this is before lawyers, of course) in an attempt to restore the child's sight, assisted in the procedure by Superman's X-ray vision.

The little girl regains her sight and flies around the world with Superman. When they fly back through the window of her New York apartment, Mom and Dad are there holding hands like young lovers. (Superman has already found Dad and brought them together with the hope that they will reconcile if given a little interval of time.) Sigh. Another half hour of fantasy with the requisite happy ending.

As I finished telling the story, coming out of my sleep-deprived haze, I turned to the mother and said, "I have no idea why I just told you that." As I gazed at her, I noticed that standing to her right was none other than George Reeves as Superman! "I must be delusional," I thought, but there he was, a three-dimensional hologram, his red cape flapping in a non-existent breeze. I could have reached out and touched him. A beam of light traveled from his eyes to the little girl sitting on my exam table. With my inner sight, assisted by Superman, I saw a dark blockage of energy deep within the area of the brain that houses the connections for the optic nerve.

I've been used to strange things happening in my practice. In fact, I have come to rely upon incidences of intuition, "magic," or the seemingly miraculous to occur. But this was a little over the top, even for me! In my vision I saw a yellow ray streaming forth from Superman's eyes. Yes, I know X-rays can't be seen by the naked eye, but I had to be able to see the energy in order to know that something was happening. I decided that whether this was a powerful hallucination, a messenger, or something from *The X-Files*, it was obviously important. I resolved to pay close attention and do whatever seemed to be the most likely course of action.

I slowly realized that there was no way to reach the blockage. I couldn't get to it, and I doubted that the girl's mother would let me drill. I briefly considered using an intra-oral cranial technique, where you put your hand in the mouth and lift up on the plates of the skull to move it in that direction. That might have worked except that she was a three-year-old. I knew from a painful experience with my own son that if you stick your hand in a child's mouth it can scare them, and in response they tend to bite.

As I checked my conceptual bag of doctor's skills, I discerned no likely alternative. Maybe I was crazy, but I decided to go with the game plan of the big guy in blue with the red cape. I am a bit of a pragmatist, and weird or not, if an event like this occurs I know there is a good reason for it. I usually just go with my gut instinct, which in this case was fairly screaming at me to pay close attention and try something new.

I placed my right hand with index finger extended on the little girl's brow, right at the location where Superman's laser beam eyes were directing me. Suddenly, a beam of energy shot out of my hand, penetrated into her skull, and flashed into the area where I had intuitively noted the energy blockage. The blockage dissolved instantly! I could see this surging energy streak all the way across the terrain of her temporal lobes, into the occipital region of her brain. It then flowed down the neurological pathways involved with the processing of visual information.

Having completed its journey, this mysterious energy turned and shot back the way it had just traveled, coming to rest at the optic chiasm where the visual pathways from the eyes intersect. The child's eyes appeared to glitter and sparkle, and a moment later she proclaimed, "There are two of you!" Acting on a clinical hunch, I performed a visual test called "accommodation," and confirmed what I had suspected; she was seeing normally for the first time. All evidence of the "lazy eye" had vanished. As strange as this tale may sound, this marked the birth of what later came to be called Matrix Energetics.

An Answer to a Prayer

Just because the energy I call Matrix Energetics discovered me, or I appear to be the one who made it up, this doesn't in any way suggest that this ability wasn't in the universe long before my experience in 1997. Countless energetic forces pass through our bodies and energy fields at every moment of our lives. We may not have developed the sensory acuity necessary to detect them with our physical senses, but that doesn't mean they are not there.

At this very moment, how many frequencies or bandwidths are passing right through our bodies? Think about it. There are radio broadcasts, TV programs, cell phone conversations, and microwave transmissions all around us, to name just a few. Information, in the form of frequencies and waves, continually inundates us. In order to pick up this information, all we need is a receiver apparatus and an antenna. There is evidence to suggest that the unconscious mind serves as the receiver and our electromagnetic field functions as the antenna. Our need or desire acts as a force of attraction, which programs our awareness to seek out experiences or information. That's one reason I think the experience of what I have chosen to call Matrix Energetics happened to me. I had a desperate need and a burning desire, and I called out to the heavens for assistance. Something heard and responded in a way I never could have imagined.

What I had been doing in my chiropractic practice at the time was no longer working very well for me. My hands had been mysteriously cramping, to the point where my fingernails sometimes dug deep into my palms. It was getting harder with each passing day to work with my hands to adjust people's spines. I prayed for help to the angels and guardians who seem to have always hovered near me, and are unfailingly present in my times of need.

When the answer to my supplications came, it was in a form that I never would have consciously imagined. I just wanted my hands to quit curling into knotted fists so that I could go about my job of being a chiropractor. What I received instead was the answer to why my hands were responding as they were. Apparently, this new energy was trying to manifest through me, and perhaps, in some unconscious manner, I was blocking its flow and the full expression of its purpose. I had asked for my hands to stop hurting. The answer was for me to open to and embrace the special qualities of this energy flowing through me.

The Guardians of Matrix Energetics

My journey toward Matrix Energetics and my current life's mission probably began one October afternoon when I was ten years old. It was mid-afternoon, right after school on a Friday. I had gone to the local drugstore to buy a comic book. Having exited the double swinging glass doors of the store, I waited patiently at the crosswalk of the busy intersection for the traffic light to change.

The walk sign flashed as I stepped off the curb. A car ran the red light and came careening toward me. I turned my head toward the sound of the racing engine and planted my feet, trying to decide which way I should run to get out of the way. The car struck me full force at chest level. The impact launched me off of my feet. I flew backward through the air, my face toward the sky, spine arched in extension.

Time almost seemed to stop. I was calm and felt no sense of fear. I recall the wind whipping around my face and the scenery going by like time-lapse photography. I felt totally at peace in the grip of what I would now define as an altered state of consciousness. At the moment before impact on the hard asphalt road, a voice that would be a harbinger of future events spoke loudly and clearly within my head. It said, *"Slap the mat!"*

Without conscious thought, I tucked my chin hard against my chest, flexed my arms at my elbows, and at the last moment extended my arms palms down, slapping the pavement in exactly the manner I would learn years later in Judo class. But how did I know in that moment what "slap the mat" meant, and how did I know to instantly respond to the urgent command of the powerful and somehow familiar voice that had commanded my attention, saving my life? Perhaps through a gracious helping of guardian angels? Or, perhaps I was tuning in to a universal knowledge of such things?

Years later, I had another strange and time-distorting incident with a distinctively martial arts flavor. It happened in seventh grade on the asphalt playground of my Catholic parochial school, Our Lady of Perpetual Help. My school experience was more like Our Lady of Perpetual Harassment. Kids at any age can be mean to each other, and the bullies and braggarts who perpetuate the mythic underpinnings of the grade school experience seem bound to pounce with fervor on any perceived weakness in a schoolmate. My class of peers decided I should be singled out in the pecking order for special attention, since I was both inordinately shy and intelligent. Well, okay... I was a bookworm nerd.

This special treatment had been visited on me for a number of years. Looking back on those times from the safety of my present perch, I realize that I might as well have painted a target on my face that read,

"Be mean to me, I won't object." I had somehow developed the mistaken impression that because I was enrolled in a religious school, I should be meek and humble, love my enemies, and turn the other cheek. I was the perfect sport for a certain class of boy who majors in petty acts of meanness. Well, that was about to change forever.

During recess on the playground my tormentors were engaged in a lively game of soccer. To this day I do not know what possessed me to volunteer to play. Not being what you would call the athletic type, I had never participated in school sports. It was out of character, to say the least, for me to overcome my timidity and ask to participate in the afternoon soccer match. It was also out of character for my classmates to somewhat graciously allow me to play. Something was up.

I began to play and in my only deft sports moment in history, and to my utter amazement, I captured the ball away from the captain of the soccer team. He fell to the ground, landing on his chin and grazing his face along the tarry surface of the hot, hard asphalt. His face burning with acute embarrassment and a cold fury, he rose to his feet and rushed at me with his hand balled into a fist. I gulped once and prepared to experience pain. Raising my arms toward my face, I cowered behind my hands in a feeble attempt to fend off the brunt of the coming blow. Then something completely unexpected and magical occurred.

Time slowed way down (again), as I watched the enraged bull charge very slowly toward me. As the extended arm of my attacker came closer, I was seized with a strange inner confidence and ability that nothing in my previous experience could have foreshadowed.

I had all the time I could ever need. My hand rose up of its own accord, palm intercepting and seizing the fist that was hurtling toward my face. With precision and grace, I caught the fist in my outstretched palm, allowing the momentum of his punch to continue forward. I sidestepped and simultaneously dropped my leading shoulder, deflecting the momentum of his swing.

10

Next, I pivoted smartly on my heel. As his arm passed over my lowered shoulder, I simultaneously turned into his body, lifted him up, and threw him expertly to the ground. My assailant lay stunned, his outstretched arm still in my hand. Taking a quick step forward, I planted my right heel against his throat. My impromptu *kata* now completed, time suddenly sped up again, and I found myself staring down at the somewhat bewildered face of my would-be attacker.

Graciously, I bent over to help him to his feet, as a shocked and perplexed throng looked on. Undoubtedly furious at this unexpected turn of affairs, he punched me in the face and stalked off, to accompanying boos from the spectators. This incident spelled the end of his popularity, and signified the dawning of a whole new chapter in my life.

Later that day, some girls in my class looked in my locker and discovered a book on *Ju Jitsu* by the popular author, Bruce Tegner. From that moment on, no one ever picked on me again. Rumors quickly spread that I had been secretly studying karate for a long time. Well, every dog has its day. I wonder what they would have said if they knew that I had bought that book two days before the incident and had not even cracked the cover?

One More Lesson

As if the previous two episodes weren't enough to get my attention, I was certainly awakened to the powerful forces at work in my life during the next strange event that happened to me. It was just after four in the morning on a bitterly cold January day in Bozeman, Montana. I did not want to get out of bed. Quickly, I went through the arguments for and against what I knew I had to do. *Let me see now, I am nearly broke, my kids are hungry, the light bill is past due, and I am not yet seeing enough patients in Bozeman to support my less-than-extravagant lifestyle. I'm definitely not a member in good standing at the local country club.*

The wind was blowing hard, and a solid sheet of glistening snow was steadily falling. It was not an ideal day for a six-hour road trip to

11

beautiful, if rustic, Missoula. But my contacts there had booked a solid weekend of clients for me. I was quite likely to make more money this weekend than I had made in the entire previous week. In my previous incarnation as a professional musician I had never missed a single gig, and I wasn't going to start now. The show must go on. That issue decided, I wearily pulled on my jeans and sweater and went to the closet for my heavy coat and snow boots.

As I left, my wife called out to me, "Be careful of black ice!" I had never seen black ice so I didn't believe in it. Shrugging off her caution and resolving not to be late, I put my foot down on the gas, and my vintage 327-cubic-inch engine and I surged uncertainly forward down the deserted highway. *Thank God the roads are empty. I should be able to make up some time on the long straight stretches of road that lie ahead of me.*

Just outside Butte, I encountered the very phenomena that my wife was always worrying about: the legendary, slippery, and all but invisible black ice. Not only did I belatedly discover the reality of its -existence, but a patch of the stuff on an icy bridge just outside Butte's city limits had my name on it. I barreled headlong toward my destiny at a speed in excess of 80 miles per hour. With the great time I was making, I'd be in Missoula soon. But then my tires started across the patch of slippery death that had formed in the center of the bridge. Horrified, I felt my wheels begin to skid out of control. In a panic, I took my foot off the gas and gently pumped the brake pedal, but I was moving too fast.

I frantically applied my brakes more forcibly, fishtailing the back end of my car so that I was now racing head-on for the bridge's pylons. I looked down at my speedometer seconds before impact and noted that it showed a crisp and lethal 65 miles per hour. I was staring death in the face and it was grinning back at me. Accepting my fate and abandoning all illusion of control, I put my hands up to my face and screamed with all of my heart, "Archangel Michael, help!" Then I hit the pillars of the bridge.

There was a blinding flash of electric blue light and then nothing. I felt as if I were floating, suspended in a big blue bubble of protective energy so thick that no harm could befall me. Archangel Michael is the defender of the faithful and the protector of the innocent. I believe in the concept of Grace, and perhaps my earthly allotment of this precious quality was not yet used up. Whatever the reason, I found myself sitting in my still-running car, in the middle of nowhere on an icy stretch of bridge, completely unharmed!

After several minutes, I recovered enough to take stock of my situation. Trying to open the driver's side door, I discovered that it was tightly crumpled, so I had to roll down the window and climb out. I was shocked to see that my whole front end was crushed up toward my windshield. It was the dead of winter on a deserted snowy road, and no one else appeared to have been so foolish as to drive in these conditions. If my car would not run, I would probably perish anyway, as the wind chill index had driven the temperature down to fifteen degrees below zero. I wondered if my life had been saved from certain death so that I could slowly freeze to death. *"That's very funny, God; I love you too!"*

Resigned to deal with whatever came next, I climbed back through the car window, slid behind the wheel, and put the car in reverse. I held my breath in fearful anticipation. The wheels spun a little bit and then, finding a purchase on the slippery road, I backed up and threw the transmission into drive, continuing on my appointed rounds. I arrived without further incident at my destination and went to work.

When it was time for the return journey home I pulled into a gas station and filled up the gas tank. Other than that, I could do little else to check the serviceability of my vehicle, as the hood of my car was so thoroughly crumpled and mangled that I doubted it would ever open again. Trusting that divine intervention was working well so far, I drove home to Bozeman, silently entreating the class of angels who doubled as car mechanics to hold the car together just a little while longer. I pulled into my driveway, and just before I turned the key, the car's engine seized up and sputtered to a stop for the last time. The car was such a total wreck that I later had to have it towed away for scrap metal. Once again, my guardian angels had come through on my behalf, and gratitude doesn't begin to cover how I felt—and continue to feel!

A State of Being

Our culture has taken things such as near-death experiences and mystical encounters, and shunted them off to the side where they can be avoided by normal consensus reality. Typically, the Western medical attitude toward people who see visions is to prescribe drugs designed to curtail that state of altered awareness so that they will fit in with the expectations of polite society. Contrast this with shamanic cultures and traditions, where you might ingest sacred substances to induce an altered state in order to divine your life's purpose. An encounter with an angel in that reality is encouraged as a normal part of life.

When I was in Bastyr getting my ND degree, I took a course called "Abnormal Psychology." We were studying schizophrenia and so-called delusional states, talking about how hearing voices in your head was a bad thing and to be avoided. I raised my hand to ask a question. My professor looked up from the assigned reading and acknowledged me with a bit of a grimace. Alas, he knew me well. Not wanting to disappoint his expectations, I innocently asked, "I hear voices in my head—and they told me to go back to school and get my Naturopathy degree. Does this mean I am schizo-something or another? Should I have opted instead to ingest a course or two of psychotropic meds?"

A grin broke through his usual sardonic manner as he replied, "No, that's probably just normal for you, if any such term applies in your case." What could be more normal or sane than listening to the voice of inner wisdom as if your life may depend on it? I can tell you from experience that sometimes it does. What do you think would have happened to Moses when he heard the voice of God speaking from the burning bush if there had been psychiatrists traveling with the tribe of Israel? Contemplate that for a while. Can't you just see it? The tribal psychiatrist learns that Moses is hearing voices again and prescribes some noxious plant root, or mercury, or whatever was available to them at that time to make the voices to stop. I *wander* where that would have led: certainly not to the land of milk and honey.

To use Matrix Energetics you do not need to have had such non-consensual experiences. Superman does not need to appear, you do not have to be clairvoyant, and you do not need to have a near-death experience. All you need is to shift the way you see and experience reality around you. The practice of Matrix Energetics is a state of being, not a technique. You can use techniques to measure and track what you are doing, but the key element is tapping into the matrix and holding the state of possibility. Sounds easy—yes? Believe me, it is remarkably easy to do. But first you must be able to experience a new possibility that will counteract the years of conditioning that you have experienced by living in this world.

2

The Medical Problem-Set

WHEN YOU GO TO SEE THE DOCTOR, one of the first things the doctor says is, "What seems to be the problem today?" Your brain goes on a search for the laundry list of everything that is currently wrong with you, or has been in the past, and then selects one or more complaints that seem appropriate. If you are seeing a chiropractor, for example, you might come up with only the information that seems relevant to the perceived purpose of the visit. You might tell the doctor how your lower back aches when you get up in the morning. But perhaps you forget to mention other medical tidbits, such as having a hundred seizures a day, or the two-pound tumor growing on the side of your foot. Well, okay, maybe not the last one; I would notice the strange choice of footwear. The point is, we delete information from our litany of complaints. Including, sadly, the last time we actually felt good!

We don't get that much practice in the art of feeling good because our whole medical system is predicated on the treatment of disease, not wellness care. Medical practice is all about identifying symptoms, conditions, and treatment: seeing you as a person with problems. This process allows doctors to figure out which little reality box we can squeeze you into. And each time you're given a different diagnosis or explanation for why you have your symptoms, it further limits your awareness of what's possible. You're stuffed into smaller and smaller boxes, where you can do less and less about more and more. Pretty soon you feel restricted, despondent, and disempowered.

We have amazingly low expectations for what we think we can get back from the universe or out of life. Our experiences will conform very closely to the structure of our beliefs about life. Often, in an effort to make progress, we end up going around in circles. Many forms of treatment or therapy seem to reinforce the problem mind-set, despite good intentions.

The Problem with Problem-Sets

The other day a new client asked me what I thought about the medical condition that another practitioner had diagnosed. I replied, "I don't know what to think about that. Whatever your doctor thinks about your condition is based upon his education and his clinical experience." She replied, "But what do you think about what he said? After all, you are a doctor as well."

Her statement gave me a moment of serious pause as I thought about what to say. I have been noticing for some time how powerful our minds really are. Current science accepts that the act of observing something, at least at the subatomic level, changes the behavior and characteristics of the thing observed. This implies that consciousness has a direct and observable affect on the structure or composition of matter. This has been borne out in so many classic experiments in quantum physics that it is now considered a fundamental principle.

At the level of the photon, consciously directed intent can alter the behaviors of the fundamental constituents of matter. If this concept is true for the photon, then it logically follows that this might be true for us as well. After all, if we accept the implications of this model, then we have to ask ourselves what humans are composed of. Photons are the smallest unit of matter that we currently recognize. Basically, when we talk about photons, we are talking about light and information.

So, in *light* of this, you may begin to understand a little more about my concerns regarding the ultimate usefulness of working professionally from the reality model of "doctor." A doctor is someone who is paid to look at you as a collection of symptoms or problems, which according to a strict professional code of conduct must be listed, described, and diagnosed, ruling out the most serious or life-threatening problems first through the appropriate tests and procedures. Inherent in the diagnosis approach is that you must then "do something." You must institute a plan of action, take a prescription, or undergo therapy (or even surgery) to address the symptoms your doctor has artfully corralled into one or more diagnoses of a disease or disorder. The diagnosis is, in part, driven by what the medical industry will accept as proof that the physician is performing his or her service, according to what is standard and customary, as agreed to by the guidelines and parameters set by each medical profession. Descriptions of what diagnoses are acceptable, and therefore reimbursable, are in part generated by the big-monied interests of the pharmaceutical corporate giants.

Medicine Wheel: We Go Round and Round

When you look at an intake history on a new patient form there is a section where the client tells you about his or her reason for consulting you. This section contains all of the information about what I have chosen to call the "problem-set" from the individual's perspective. Unfortunately, to complicate this process further and to make it thoroughly vulnerable to the principles of quantum entanglement, this section also often contains information as well as previous diagnostic prognostications from other health care professionals. This fact can make for what I clinically call "a snarly mess."

Consider the case of a poor medical student (let's call her Donna) who consults a naturopath, Dr. Dave, for complaints of fatigue, weight gain, and problems with digestion. Coincidentally, Dr. Dave had an experience when he was in medical school in which he developed, probably due to the stress of his constant workload, the following symptoms: fatigue, abdominal distension, and the tendency to incompletely digest his meals.

Dr. Dave's doctor performed a standard panel of blood tests and found nothing wrong, according to the test results. She prescribed digestive enzymes and suspected that perhaps Dave had undiagnosed food allergies. As part of the general protocol taught at her medical school, Dave was prescribed a strict rotation diet eliminating wheat, chocolate, caffeine, and a lot of other tasty, fun foodstuffs that are the most common offenders when food allergies are suspected. Having had this experience, Dr. Dave prescribes a similar treatment to our medical student, Donna.

Donna dutifully sticks to this strict regimen for three months, experiencing some change in her overall energy level, but is still bothered by the abdominal bloating and distension. Dissatisfied by the modest level of her results, she decides to see another clinician. This time, a lab test is run for a thyroid profile. Although the test results come back within normal range—in other words, no clinical evidence of pathology—the clinician has just attended a seminar on functional endocrine disturbances, and therefore decides that Donna's symptoms are consistent with a functional endocrine disorder. He prescribes an herbal formula designed to tonify her thyroid. This seems to help with Donna's overall level of energy and she is able to get through her day without feeling so exhausted.

However, all too soon it becomes apparent that the weight loss is just not happening. Returning to the clinic, she sees a new clinician who, on top of running the same blood tests as before, decides to include an allergy panel for IgA-reactive foods. This test comes back showing that Donna demonstrates, according to the results, a number of significant allergies and she must immediately eliminate all of the offending foods from her diet. In fact, a raw food diet with lots of fresh vegetable juices is just the thing for her. (This clinician couldn't sleep last night, and happened to watch a high-energy infomercial on the benefits of juicing. He is gung-ho to do this for himself.)

After a few days on the new regimen Donna again feels more energy, but she notices that now she is experiencing a lot of gas and distension after meals. Hearing good things about another practitioner, Dr. Tom, who does muscle testing for allergies, Donna decides to see what Dr. Tom can do for her. According to Dr. Tom's muscle tests, she has lots of allergies: not to worry, Dr. Tom can "fix" her. It is a simple matter of a mere twenty-eight visits to the expensive tune of two visits per week. "You must understand," Dr. Tom tells her, "in order to fix these allergies, you must submit to a rigid protocol, which is guaranteed to work if you do exactly as I say."

Weary now of the doctor merry-go-round, Donna tells Dr. Tom that she will consider it, but she doesn't have the money to start the treatment plan right now. Dr. Tom responds with, "Okay, it is your decision, but just remember that if you delay proper treatment, things will only get worse." Thanking Dr. Tom, Donna leaves his office more confused than ever, but determined to get to the bottom of her health issues. Deeply disheartened, she resolves to go to a "real" medical doctor to get a more traditional assessment and workup.

The medical doctor repeats the same blood tests and tells Donna that there is nothing wrong with her. All of her blood labs fall within normal limits. *As if that tells her anything constructive; perhaps it is normal to feel the way that she does.* But in addition, he pokes at Donna's body in a number of places, nodding to himself occasionally, as if confirming his clinical suspicions. Finally, he shares with her the result of his cursory exam, telling her that it is as he thought. The test where he has poked and prodded her in seventeen different places confirms the diagnosis. Donna has Fibromyalgia! Her newly acquired medical professional explains to her how all of her symptoms fit the diagnostic criteria for Fibromyalgia.

This "diagnosis" includes symptoms of widespread musculoskeletal pain. Sometimes the muscles twitch, sometimes they burn. Some people just say they hurt all over like they have the flu. One of the symptoms sufferers are commonly plagued with is pain *(dig the cool hypnotic language patterns which will have you feeling worse at any moment)*. This pain is described as deep, reeeally deep nooowww, the medical hypnotist intones, and can include stabbing and shooting pains; why all of the violent metaphors? Included on this laundry list is intense, burning pain. *This could really be a problem if you had the misfortune of going to a psychic and being told that in a previous life you were burned at the stake for being a witch!*

Fatigue is another symptom that is very common with this syndrome, ranging from mild fatigue to total incapacitation. Some people even report a kind of brain fog, which makes them feel drained of energy. Donna nods in response to this continuing onslaught of information, *or is she just beginning to nod off?* Put yourself in her place, as she continues to listen to the doctor's information, and see how you begin to feel.

Associated with this syndrome is a cluster of other conditions, such as headaches, migraine headaches, irritable bowel syndrome *(a syndrome within a syndrome?)*, TMJ dysfunction, sleep disorders, PMS, chest pain, morning stiffness, memory problems, irritable bladder, dry eyes and mouth, dizziness, impaired coordination, *as well as a profoundly decreased ability to detect medical dumping grounds for collections of symptoms which may not measure up to the criteria for actually having a discrete disease entity!*

In addition, there are aggravating factors *(you mean besides doctors?)*, changes in weather, and allergies. *Uh-oh, here we are back at the beginning of this medical Mobius strip!* Cold or drafty environments, hormonal fluctuations—darn, I still think something is wrong with my thyroid. Stress, depression, over-exertion, and anxiety, *like maybe right now, listening to all of this* can lead to flare-ups. *There are flares going up all around me right now: "Danger Will Robinson!"* "Now, I think that is all relatively clear. Do you have any questions for me?" says the doctor kindly. *Yes, can you call someone who will take me to my sick bed? I suddenly feel very ill!*

Now comes the good part. Remember what I have already said about how diagnosis must always be followed by some form of prescription or treatment? Here is a real doozy: medical treatment for Fibromyalgia Syndrome, or FMS, typically includes some form of prescription antidepressant such as Prozac, or a similar brand of neurochemical stew. I have often said that FMS might best properly stand for "Forget Medical Suggestions." If the average person had to sit through an examination with the doctor describing all of what I have just related, the internally loaded images of illness alone would practically ensure a less-than-favorable prognosis.

In addition to the already dismal clinical picture that has just been narrated to the hapless patient, Fibromyalgia is often coupled with another condition called functional sleep apnea, which means that when you sleep, your brain is deprived of adequate oxygen levels for brief periods of time intermittently throughout the night. This condition can be diagnosed by subjecting you to a "sleep study" at a licensed clinic specializing in sleep disorders.

And here is the really good news; your insurance will pay the doctors for this test, which (*surprise*) almost always proves that you have the problem. In addition, once diagnosed, the treatment involves an expensive contraption that you must wear all night. The apparatus ensures that your brain receives adequate levels of oxygen. The good news here, of course, is that your insurance will usually pay for this treatment as well. I wonder how many people, out of a random sample, would demonstrate positive for this problem if tested?

Look at all of the observers who are now entangled with Donna's symptoms. These ghosts of practitioners are trailing along with her. Does this sound hauntingly familiar? Each previous observer has held these conditions up as problems, giving them even more strength and power. As you study Matrix Energetics, you will see that shifting your perspective out of the problem-set and into one of many possibilities or the "solution-set" is often all that is needed to affect lasting transformations in your health and in all aspects of your life.

The "Do Something!" Disease

What is wrong with a stimulus/response model for the practice of medicine? Nothing, other than that the very consciousness behind how it is practiced ensures that we are always caught in a loop of cause and effect, which once begun has no end and becomes self-perpetuating like some insane version of a Mobius strip. We are firmly in the grips of what Dr. Robert S. Mendelsohn (*Confessions of a Medical Heretic*) humorously referred to as the dreaded "do something disease." How many of you have a spouse or significant other who has goaded you into an ill-conceived response to an event by stating imperatively, "Don't just stand there! Do something!" In my personal life at least, nothing good has ever come of my reflex responses in such a situation.

3

Solutions, Not Problems

YOUR PERCEPTIONS WILL CONTROL YOUR REALITY. Chapter 4 will outline some of the science behind this statement, but by now I hope you're getting the idea that the medical problem-set is not the best reality to play in. Let me give you a simple example of what I mean.

If I were to lift a fairly heavy object without bending my knees, as we have all been programmed not to do, I might injure myself and be diagnosed with a muscle strain of the back. Say I then chat with my neighbor over the backyard fence and he tells me, "Oh, that is a really bad sprain. I know all about that. One time I hurt my back so badly that I could barely get out of bed for two weeks! Those things can take months to heal. Sometimes, I was told by one of my therapists, they never heal completely at all. Nothing was ever the same after I did that to my back." If I buy into my neighbor's reality completely, then I will certainly follow the same path of healing as he did. If I take his experience "lying down," then I have made my bed—and I guess I will just have to lie in it. I will now have one very limiting set of beliefs about my condition.

Look at All Your Solutions

If you consider yourself to be a healer, I wish to get one thing out of the way so that we are clear. All techniques work within the confines of the reality subset for which they were constructed. As long as you agree to cooperate within the rules that the technique founder has provided, you will remain safely congruent with the types of results that they describe. It is when you begin to look outside of the parameters of the system's preloaded, prefabricated reality filters that you may run into some trouble.

I personally practice an eclectic approach to my own health care. I will still use an aspirin on occasion if I have a headache. When I have been really down-and-out sick, I have resorted to a prescription antibiotic if the so-called "natural" approaches didn't cut it. I am not a fanatic about any of this. Although I have earned two medical degrees, something that is even more important to me is the following idea: *How many degrees of freedom does what I am doing and thinking afford to me?* At any moment, I want to be able to choose, rather than to find myself locked into some form of conceptual prison of my own making.

We all, in each moment of life, do the best that we can do in that moment. If I am not feeling very resourceful in the present moment, I see no problem with considering all of my alternatives and keeping my options open. Not all surgery is bad. Drugs can be necessary and helpful for some people. Just because Matrix Energetics flows through me twenty-four hours a day does not mean I stop respecting, or even utilizing, whatever else is out there.

Be Aware of What Your Solution Implies

Keep in mind that when you treat symptoms or conditions, you are choosing to participate, albeit sometimes wisely, in the "us vs. them" mentality, which by and large characterizes the identity of medical thinking and practice. And there is nothing wrong with this. Just recognize the limitations inherent within the model, and respect and honor it for what it is and what it does extremely well. If you break your leg, you are going to want and need a crutch. However, if you wish to break ingrained habits of thinking, you would want to dispense with ideological crutches.

Every treatment in medicine, including most so-called natural alternatives, is in reaction to a symptom or condition. This symptom/treatment duality means that you have this condition (symptom), and I am going to prescribe treatment for that condition. It is a stimulus-response or behaviorist model at its core, largely extrapolated from laboratory studies on rats. But how many of you reading this think rat physiology and biochemistry are close enough to those of human beings that our medical healthcare should be based on them?

One of the greatest problems that I have noticed in the treatment of symptoms from within this stimulus-response model is that anything you do in reaction to a condition tends to add energy into sustaining the unwanted state. If you address a condition by treating it, you devote more attention to its existence, thus validating its reality. When you do this you make the condition itself more linear, predictable, and ultimately more self-aware. That, I am sure, is exactly what we don't want: for our conditions to become more self-aware!

An Alternative to the "Us vs. Them" Approach

In contrast with the above approach, when I work with people, they often have a hard time describing what I did or what happened. Initially, they may not even be sure that anything did occur, save for the fact that when I wave my hand close to their body, they suddenly wind up unconscious on the floor. Better yet, they find themselves curled into some self-inflicted body pose, which often appears uncannily similar to what you might see in yoga or qigong postures. The fact that this happens automatically and with no previous experience with me often clinches the deal in their minds that something unusual has just occurred. You want something that you cannot make sense of or encode in the same old ways. If you can't make sense of your experience, perhaps you won't be able to put it back together in exactly the same old way.

I do not use Matrix Energetics as a clinical tool that I pull out of my bag of tricks to do battle with some kinds of disease. Inherently, it is best not used in an us vs. them mind-set. This is primarily because anything that you perceive and observe from a framework based in duality can reinforce the strength of the condition you find yourself battling. I point out to people that this approach to health and disease firmly affixes your experience in particle-based or consensus reality. I practice a different approach, in that I observe the person as being in a fluid or wavelike consciousness state. To my way of thinking, the human body is made of photons. From this quantum perspective I have more leverage from which to assist you in transforming your life.

By seeing in this manner, you are able to engage your consciousness in a reality subset that allows you to utilize a number of peculiar advantages. Once you do this, theoretically you can intercept a condition or trauma at or just before its inception, and observe the outcome as being different. In this way, you can engage a new set of probability outcomes, potentially changing the manifestation of your conditions and problems.

How Do Problem-Sets Get to Be Such Problems?

I believe that the consciousness that goes into creating any condition or concept creates its own "Morphic Field," so named by biologist Rupert Sheldrake. What Sheldrake postulates is that for each species there are group energy fields that are held as a group awareness, or a morphogenetic field. From a consciousness model or perspective, whenever you start to add new information or learning to the data banks of a specific morphic field, a certain critical mass can be reached at some evolutionary point. At this point of critical mass, an entire species can become simultaneously aware of a new pattern of information or behaviors; this feedback system is known as morphic resonance, or popularly, as the so-called hundredth monkey effect.

The name "hundredth monkey" refers to what researchers saw happening when a species of monkey on an isolated island learned a new behavior: in this case, washing the sand off a potato before ingesting it. At some critical mass, when enough monkeys on the island had learned to do this, suddenly and simultaneously on the other outlying islands, the monkeys of the same species spontaneously began washing their potatoes in exactly the same manner. Although this report was actually determined to be speculation and not observation on the part of the researchers, it was originally published as factual. In spite of attempts to clarify the misinformation, the hundredth monkey effect has become a cultural parable that has propagated in a manner not unlike morphic resonance itself.

A similar study occurred with a species of white rat that was bred over many generations to run a maze that had been immersed in water. The initial groups of rats took a very long time to learn the swimming skills that the researchers taught to them. I don't know how long it took on the average, and the life expectancy of a rat in a lab is probably brief. When the rats succeeded in learning the task, the scientists would sacrifice them by cutting into their brains to see if there were notable changes in their cyto-architecture. Talk about a motivation-killing behavior!

Over the generations, as the rats were born and set up to run the maze of their predecessors, it was discovered that though they had never seen the maze, all of the rats of that species in all of the labs across the country could, on their first attempt, swim the maze as well as, or better than, the trained rats of the previous generation. Eventually, to the surprise of the researchers, all of the rats of this same species were born with the inherent ability to run the maze, even if their ancestors had never been trained in a lab to be able to perform this task.

I have made an intuitive leap, which I must confess is not well supported by the body of research derived from the systematic torture of rats. I was once asked by one of my professors if what I was telling him about a particular clinical subject consisted of my own ideas, or if it was supported by research. I replied to him that my thoughts were my own, and that instead of going over the same often tired old areas of thinking that research can represent, I preferred to have ideas that no one had thought of before. In other words, instead of research, I preferred "search." So, you have been warned that what I am about to share are my thoughts alone, and I have sole responsibility for their content.

The Good Thing About Morphic Fields

The idea of morphic resonance postulates that for each species, DNA acts as a tuner, which receives instructions for the correct type and components for that biological entity from the energy of the morphogenetic field. Scientists acknowledge that weak electromagnetic fields surround the biological organism, and indeed are given off by every component, down to the smallest atomic structure. In the morphogenetic model, the field *in-forms* the DNA hardware what to make from its instructions. The field is the blueprint, as Harold Saxton Burr suggested in his book, *The Fields of Life: Our Links with the Universe*.

Rupert Sheldrake wrote about this in a fascinating series of articles in the magazine *Psychological Perspectives*, Spring 1987, one of which was entitled "Mind, Memory, Archetype: Morphic resonance and the collective unconscious."

Sheldrake points out in one article that if you are watching television you do not assume that the tiny pictures you see on the screen are actually generated by the components of the television set. It has a tuner, which homes in on the correct frequency or channel and allows your TV set to pick up the program. If you damage the components of the set you merely interrupt its ability to receive the field or pattern of information that is carried on the electromagnetic field of the program's signal.

Sheldrake explains that if you chop up a magnet you will have a lot of little magnets that generate their own fields. Fields are associated with the properties of life. Each organ, tissue, cell, and structure has its own associated field. It is the field, Sheldrake believes, that determines what organs form and what qualities and characteristics they express. In his view, you have the characteristics and looks of your parents not from their DNA, which is the hardware, but rather, you *download* your general biological traits from the collective field of the human race. The individual characteristics and quirks of your body/mind are derived, at least in part, from your parents' specific morphic fields. It is the blueprint or conceptualization of the Master Architect that provides the template for the "house of clay" to be built.

Sheldrake links the idea of morphic fields to the concept of archetypes introduced by Carl Jung. "If there is an oak tree, then there is an archetypal pattern or form which represents the oak tree," Sheldrake writes. He postulates that the collective unconscious of humanity provides a background base for the collective memory of humanity. "What I am suggesting is that a very similar principle operates throughout the entire universe, not just in human beings."

Sheldrake has postulated that morphic fields influence everything from plant growth, to the migratory patterns of birds, to what Carl Jung called "the collective unconscious." Sheldrake writes, "The whole point about morphic fields is that nature as we know it is mutable and adaptable. Anything which influenced or imposed a pattern upon chance could bring about a causative influence in nature not violating any of the laws of physics."

I am also fond of a university study that Sheldrake refers to. In it, day-old chicks were put in the same room with a robot that had a picture of a mother hen on it. The robot had been programmed to move randomly; however, when the baby chicks looked at it, the randomness was disrupted. When observed by the baby chicks, the robot's patterns of movement deviated toward the chicks to a statistically significant degree. Apparently, as I suspected in my pre-adolescent teens, chicks may rule the universe.

Following his ideas wherever they might point, Sheldrake boldly portrays the power of social and spiritual ritual as a way to initiate, build, and sustain a collective morphic field. "In general, rituals are highly conservative in nature and must be performed in the right way, which is the same way that they have been performed in the past. Ritual acts must be performed with correct movements, gestures, words, and music throughout the world. If morphic resonance occurs as I think it does, this conservatism of ritual would create exactly the right conditions for morphic resonance to occur between those performing the ritual now and all of those who performed it previously."

Sheldrake talks about how systems of thought may also have their own morphic fields. He points out that we do, after all, call professions the "field" of medicine, the "field" of engineering, and so forth. This makes perfect sense to me. I have discovered that if I don't know how to do a technique or system, and my client could benefit from that approach, I am able to directly access the morphic field information or abilities of the subject that I am interested in rather than take a seminar or read a book about the particular subject. I have, for instance, *borrowed* the skills of an acupuncturist in China in order to balance someone's meridians.

Is that really what I did? I don't know for certain. I mean, how can you objectively verify something like that? I do know that when I do something along these lines I usually "get" information that is specific and relevant to what I needed to know. In my seminars, I tell participants that they can "borrow" my abilities with Matrix Energetics if they want to have a powerful experience. I often close my eyes and access the intuitive skills of my friend Mark Dunn. When I do this I can "see" things clairvoyantly that would normally not present themselves to my awareness.

What I am talking about is possible—or at least it's easy to imagine that it is. Quantum science has shown that effects in the quantum realm are non-local in character. This means that the information at the level of the photon is entangled. This understanding opens the door for phenomena such as telepathy. Have you ever heard the saying, "Great minds think alike"? With what you just read about morphic resonance, you can easily begin to understand how ideas and concepts can be accessed and brought to conscious awareness from the unlimited pool of universal intelligence.

My point is that when you free up your thinking from its normal linear patterns, you can begin to access and integrate new information directly from the Zero Point Energy Field: what some physicists have referred to as the Mind of God. This is one reason I emphasize that to do Matrix Energetics you really don't have to know anything. You can know nothing while doing No thing and access the All, which is contained within the One.

I believe that systems of thought, such as healing techniques, represent their own subset of a specialized type of morphic field, and that you can use this idea to your advantage. The longer a technique has been around, and the greater the number of practitioners, the more powerfully expressive and effective that technique can be. Techniques feature stylized methodologies and beliefs, which are delivered to their adherents at the hands of the guru or founder of the particular system.

I was always told not to mix and match systems, but this never made sense to me. I am constitutionally of a stubborn and questioning nature. I am willing to take some things on faith if they deliver as promised. Results, not empty facts or theories, are really what counts in anything. If you want to follow the status quo, go right ahead. I don't want to become a statistic. If the odds are against me then I will go with the evens.

For an easy example of this, take the healing system known as Reiki. I believe some of the power that is obviously invested in the

Reiki symbols and their ability to be tapped or channeled by Reiki practitioners has a lot to do with the same concept as a morphic field. What if morphic fields were not only actively present in biological species, but in systems of thought and belief as well? Each healing system or school of thought comprises at its energetic core a very specific morphic field. Everyone who is in agreement with the consciousness of that group mind or energy will have full access to the field of information and power of that system.

Practicing Reiki, or any technique or system of healing, is a little like being Captain Kirk and having access to the tremendous power of the phaser banks of the *Enterprise*. If techniques or systems of thought and feeling actually create their own morphic fields, then once you have properly grasped them as a possible reality, for example, you as a Reiki practitioner have access to the same power. That is perhaps why so many of the technique masters emphasize obeying the rules and following them just as they do. When you enter into performing the technique or ritual wholeheartedly, you become one with the unique subset of reality that they have observed and created.

The knowledge and experiences of everyone who has ever practiced any discipline or science are available to anyone who creates a bond with that consensual reality. The key is to resonate with something so completely that you, in essence, become it. If you only do this halfheartedly, it won't work; *you must embody it*. Once you embody it, you are linked into the power grid of that morphic field, and you are in resonance with it. That is when the magic, the miraculous-appearing healing, occurs, because you are linking up with an enormous database of universal energy—and anything can happen with that.

A very powerful example of this occurred in my office recently. I have a client who has been plagued for years with a painful TMJ syndrome. Numerous dentists and orthodontic specialists have tried to fix the problem to no avail. One practitioner insisted that the solution was to surgically break her jaw in two places and then remold it. Talk about your custom bodywork! My client was assured that this was a traditional and well-accepted method of treating this problem. But she decided to make a break for it and never went back.

One day in my office she was telling me this and I was suddenly inspired by my guides. She was telling me about a new oral surgeon she had consulted for this issue. I got a really good gut feeling about him. "I can work with this guy. He knows some great stuff," I thought. My guides told me to create a template of this man's knowledge and to install that pattern in my client. Not questioning how this might be accomplished, I held my right hand up and envisioned a disc of light, or hologram, being created. When I saw and felt that it was complete I mentally released the pattern into her energy field. The results were immediate and stunning. She gently fell over onto my massage table in a deep trance.

When she came back to full conscious awareness she wore a smile as bright as the midday sun. Moving her jaw from side to side, she exclaimed, "All of the pain is gone!" Later that week she went back to the orthodontist whose knowledge and skills I had "borrowed" and he could not believe his eyes. She related that he looked first at her X-rays, and then started rapidly scanning his notes. "I don't believe it. How is this possible?" All of the clinical parameters that he had so carefully documented and outlined were gone. To this doctor's credit, he wanted to know what I had done. Unlike many of us when confronted with new information, he accepted the evidence that his eyes provided and then became curious. My client tells me that he will be sending a few test cases my way soon.

A local neurologist heard about me from some of his patients. Intrigued, he sent me a test case, a woman with a compendium of symptoms. She did not sleep well at night, and some nights barely at all. She had numerous muscular aches and pains, including a wicked case of TMJ. But the most difficult problem was a diabetic condition that was not responding to insulin. Because of the principles I teach in Matrix

Energetics, all of these symptoms rapidly improved after a few office visits. The neurologist was intrigued and decided to pay me a visit.

On a Saturday morning a handsome young man strolled into my office and heartily shook my hand. Perplexed and a bit worried about a scheduling conflict, I asked him if he was a new client. I was worried that my office had double-booked two people in the same time slot. Smiling, he informed me that he was the doctor I was expecting. Relieved and a little taken aback by this man's easygoing and pleasant nature, I clasped his hand in both of mine and warmly greeted him.

Sitting quietly in a spare chair in my treatment room, he watched with intense focus as I worked with our mutual patient. He began to tilt his head and a frown deepened across his brow. I thought, "Uh-oh, now I am in for it!" Suddenly, he sprang up from his chair and crossed the room to where I stood. With a wondering expression on his countenance, he clasped his hand to my shoulder and exclaimed, "You are manipulating quantum reality fields!" I broke into an expansive grin and replied, "Yes, I think I am. Thank you for noticing!" "Cool!" was his rejoinder.

Now here is one final story to drive home how much power and knowledge can be instantly available to you if you link up and let go of your fears and limitations. Recently, I was teaching a large seminar in San Diego and a big gentleman with an even bigger heart and smile approached me in a practice session. He embraced me warmly, and with tears in his eyes he told me this story:

"I am an orthopedic surgeon practicing in the country of Dubai near Saudi Arabia. A month ago, a friend directed me to take a look at your website. I watched your streaming video and was intrigued.

"You were demonstrating the correction of scoliosis, an abnormal curvature of the spine. I saw you touch two places with your fingertips on her back, and suddenly she appeared to faint and was gently lowered to the floor. I was amazed to see that when she stood back up the curvature in her spine was now normal! I decided that if you can do it, I can do it!

"I had a twenty-eight-year-old woman in my office who had a kypho-scoliosis (an abnormal rounded curve in her mid-spine). I touched two points on her back just as you had in your video, and she seemed to briefly go unconscious.

"Moments later, when she came to, I was shocked to discover that the condition in her spine had been completely corrected! This was a case that would have been difficult to fix with surgery. For three weeks I had her come to my office, thinking her condition might recur: It did-n't. On the fourth week she asked me what we do next, and that was all I knew. Looking on your website, I saw you were teaching in California this weekend so I hopped a plane and that is why I am here."

We both broke into tears and began bear hugging each other like long-lost brothers. He graciously told his story to everyone at the event later that day. I was overwhelmed with joy and gratitude for the grace that has allowed me to teach these concepts.

If you look through the eyes of anyone's belief system, you will only see the things that those perceptual filters allow for. In the movie *What the Bleep Do We Know!?* the story is told about when Columbus came to the New World and members of a native tribe could not see the huge ships that were anchored out in the bay, even when they were looking right at them. There was no precedent in their experience for such objects or events, so their minds deleted the visual information that did not conform to their established view of reality; it was not a part of the experience of the prevailing paradigm. The shaman of the tribe, however, could see the water disturbances, and by looking for what he did not know how to see, shifting into a state where he could see in a different way, he finally saw the ships and was then able to show the tribesmen how to see them as well.

Interestingly, author Alexandra Bruce in her fascinating book *Beyond the Bleep* states that she is surprised that this story showed up at all in the movie. Calling it a "hackneyed unsubstantiated urban leg-end," she states that no one has ever been able to trace its sources. That is probably true, but I still like the story. It is just another example of what I like to call a "useful fiction." The possibility that it is not true in no way diminishes its metaphorical value in stimulating your mind to consider the evidence of things hoped for, but not seen. If it helps you to get your "ship" together, it matters not to me one whit if it sails upon nothing more than a sea of fantasy.

Every morning I wake up and look for those ships of "state" that can only be seen when you enter a non-consensus view of reality. Every day I ask myself, "What am I not thinking or realizing, that if perceived, could alter my perspective to the benefit of all concerned?" Tony Robbins talks about the power of questions. He suggests that you have five paradigm-expanding power questions that you ask yourself every day. If you habitually ask your brain a different or more empowering question, eventually it will get with the program and start to generate more powerful answers for you.

Be Prepared to Get Crazy

We could make the case for the idea that we modern Westerners have not experienced and understood such things as the shamanic worldview, which incorporates an awareness of multiple realities that are accessible and easily navigated by the experienced shaman. To us, a journey to the lower world can only be compared to something we already accept or at least have some exposure to, such as Jung's concepts of active imagination or visualization. But to the shaman and his culture, the lower and upper worlds are key shamanic concepts, and are as real as what they call the middle world—our only recognized reality in the West.

Is it possible that someone labeled as schizophrenic and locked away from society or placed on psychoactive medications in order to enforce upon them the "correct view" of reality might be considered in another culture as having a rare and prized spiritual gift or ability? This is not to suggest that I, in any way, think that practicing shamans are schizophrenic or that schizophrenics should go off their medication and bang a drum or shake a rattle. I am merely pointing out that what seems crazy to one way of thinking might be quite a functional world-view, and even an essential skill, when playing by different rules and in the appropriate context.

What you are able to think and perceive defines the limitations of what you are able to achieve. So if you learn a particular set of rules and beliefs in a particular technique, or any adopted way of thinking, you have that technique or system's blinders on. It is an acquired set of rules that conform to your expectations. As soon as you start to question or see things from a different perspective, you run the risk of upsetting your treasured assumptions about reality. It's that same phenomenon that the physicists are still puzzling over. Why does an electron behave like a particle when you are looking at it, but assume the pattern of a wave as soon as you look at it with a different set of expectations or take your attention off it altogether? *Welcome to the Observer Effect.*

Now, if you are happy with the results that you are getting in life, and you have the ability to manifest the things that you focus on, then by all means "play on brother man," as Jimi Hendrix said. However, if you aren't satisfied with the way things are going, realize that you have the powerful ability to observe and perceive reality differently. But please don't take anything I am saying to ridiculous extremes. As with anything in life, common sense is a very helpful guideline here. If I am driving down the road in my car and traffic is whizzing by me, I don't want to suddenly decide to try to vibrate my vehicle through the back of the car in front of me. You have heard about great scientific discoveries that have occurred by accident; this is not what we are talking about here. I know that metaphysicians are fond of saying that there is no such thing as an accident, but that doesn't mean I want to personally cause one!

The Power of a Made-Up Reality

I do suggest that if you are going to observe reality in a different way, you want to make up a reality that helps people, that uplifts mankind, and that contributes to the greater good. For instance, one of the great technique masters whom I have had the honor of learning from, Dr. Victor Frank, DC, developed a reflex system of testing and treating people called Total Body Modification. It has proven itself over the last thirty years; its practitioners are able to address most of the diseases or conditions that plague mankind. He made up a reality that if he tested a reflex for the liver, and the client's indicator muscle went weak, it meant the liver had a problem.

Not content to simply understand the problem, he then devised a system of corrections, most of which are done in sequences on the spine: a different corrective sequence for each organ reflex. So, you test the liver reflex, do the technique thing, and the indicator muscle is now strong when retested. So what? It doesn't seem like much happened, except for that little glitch in consensus reality where what you just did will sometimes reverse liver disease. I do not think something like that has to happen in every instance in order for it to be statistically significant, do you?

I was at a Total Body Modification seminar where a young doctor stood up and told a story about when he had attended my basic workshop. Returning home, he found a weak prostate reflex on his dad, which was not surprising since he had recently been diagnosed with prostate cancer. The new convert to TBM did the correction indicated, and the indicator muscle showed that the prostate reflex was now "fixed." If you leave the story at that point, it is interesting but not earthshaking in its importance. Listen to the rest of the story, though, before you decide. When the doc's dad went back to the doctor, all of the tests showed that his cancer had mysteriously disappeared and his PSA values were normal, indicating a healthy prostate. Now what do you think? I think you're not in Kansas anymore, Toto.

My practice partner, Dr. Mark Dunn, looked at TBM and some of the other weird but effective techniques and thought to himself, "What quackery is this? This can't possibly work." He used to pull my patients aside when I left the room and ask them, "All right, you can tell me the truth. What is really going on?" And they would reply, "Oh, you are so lucky to be studying with him. He has helped me so much. I don't know what I would've done without him," and so forth. This stuff just made Dr. Dunn teeth-gnashing crazy. He used to come into the office in the morning and say, "Good morning. Have I told you how much I hate you today?" And I think he was only partly kidding because what he was learning from me was totally shaking up his sane, stable world, and often was in conflict with what he learned in medical school.

He watched me for nine months, initially sitting in a room with the patients and me. At some level, he probably hated every minute of it. Finally, when he started seeing his own clients, he tried TBM with someone who had an absolutely terrible chronic case of constipation. Mark thought to himself, "What do I have to lose?" So he treated the colon reflexes because they tested weak.

There is no chance that what happened next had anything to do with placebo. Dr. Dunn was absolutely convinced, and I am sure his unconscious body language communicated this to the patient's awareness, that nothing would happen. Against all expectations of either party to this unfolding drama, the client suddenly felt rumbling in her long-dormant intestines and raced to the bathroom. This concluded my friend's first personal experience of helping someone by utilizing weird or "voodoo medicine." This experience led Dr. Dunn to conclude that TBM actually stood for Totally (awesome) Bowel Movements.

The next few patients with whom he tried the same maneuver experienced no noticeable therapeutic results. He asked me what was going on, and I said I hoped he had enjoyed the honeymoon, because from here on it was all work—welcome to the frustrating world of TBM or anything else. Sometimes life is a slippery slope and we do indeed slide. Mark then did something unconsciously that I considered a brilliant way to test the reality of his therapeutic efforts; he worked so

41

hard and did so much on each visit with a client that invariably the result would be that they would throw up during the office visit. With this new development he no longer questioned that what he was doing was working; he now knew that it just was not working in the way that he wanted.

By making everyone who came to see him throw up, he unconsciously chose a safe outcome, which he could objectively verify by using his rational mind to confirm that something observable was happening. After several months, he got control over the manifestation of this unwanted side effect of his gung-ho attitude, and since that time has continually improved his skills.

I touched on something a few moments ago that I consider very important to the development of Matrix Energetics. It's somewhat like the attitude our State Department had under Ronald Reagan when working with the Soviets on arms agreements: "Trust, but verify." When working at any task, you always want a criterion to verify, "Did it do what I thought it did, or not? Is this something that I can believe and trust? Can I depend on it?" But there is a Catch-22 here, because in my experience, as long as you believe in something and trust it, then you can depend on it. This is similar to what my spiritual teachers say. There is a formula for alchemical manifestations and spiritual mastery. The catch is that once you find the formula you no longer need it, because you have become the formula in the process of your searching.

If we accept some of the current limitations imposed by the postulated laws of physics, reality is, in many ways and to a large extent, what you make of it. Or, put another way, reality as defined by you is dependent on how you choose to interact with it. You want to work with your conception of reality, to reconfigure its meaning in such a way that you begin to get reliable outcomes whenever you attempt to transform your own, or someone else's, life circumstances. The good news is that like most other things in life, you get much better at being able to do this with consistent and sustained practice. I think the more you focus your intent in highly specific ways, the more you tap into the universal power of the morphic field, which contains the energetic blueprint or matrix for the results that you want. You just have to keep rubbing and polishing that magic lamp until the genie appears.

Creating Your Own Winning Mythologies

In Matrix Energetics, as I said earlier, we do not like to work on "conditions" because doing so simply reinforces the condition. But in some instances, the shared reality of a particular condition can be a little overwhelming, such as in the case of cancer. If you think of cancer as having its own morphic field, perhaps you can begin to understand the possible magnitude of the problem. We would have to include factors such as everyone who has ever had it, every medical text or article about it that has ever been published, and every method, doctor, and institution that has been established to treat it. Plus, there are intense survival issues and beliefs about illness or death.

It is a huge field of energy and you don't want to go up against that field one-on-one. You must go outside the established rules of reality because you are not likely to win at that game. You will need to redefine the battle lines. Ideally, you do not enter into a confrontation with a condition of this magnitude at all. Dr. John Christopher, the prominent herbalist, used to say that there are no incurable conditions, but there are incurable individuals.

If a particular problem you are working with seems insurmountable, why not just change the rules a little bit and try something different that perhaps no one before you has ever thought of? Certainly, if you hear the small, still voice of intuitive guidance, and if what it suggests appears to be uplifting and helpful, then why not give the new concept a test spin? You never know; you might be on the threshold of a new reality or possibility. Perhaps you can develop a new system and become a technique guru in your own right. Change the rules so that you have the possibility of not always getting what you've always gotten.

When you learn to drive a car you realize that everyone agrees to play by a certain set of rules. Everyone agrees what a right or left turn means, although not everyone always clearly signals his or her intended direction. Similarly, there are rules for observing our reality that we all have, for the most part, clearly agreed upon. For instance, when you look down at the floor you are pretty certain that it is not likely to start melting away from beneath your feet—unless, of course, you grew up in the psychedelic era and perhaps imbibed too much of the culture of the time. Or you spend too much time looking at hotel carpet patterns!

Changing Reality the Quantum Way

Today, we understand that quantum physics is having a ripple effect on how we perceive reality. This paradigm shift in how we make up reality is exemplified in the recent documentary, *What the Bleep Do We Know!?* The traditional model of an atom's structure was very straightforward and easily comprehended. In this model, the atom was depicted with a nucleus consisting of a proton and a neutron. Around the nucleus, the electron was pictured to orbit in a more or less elliptical and very predictable orbit. But once quantum physicists began to look closely at this model, we learned that the electron doesn't actually behave in such a clear-cut manner.

Instead of acting in the sensible mathematical model that I have just discussed, it appears that the electron actually does something that is a lot more interesting, if a little difficult to conceptualize. According to a quantum model, the electron moves in probability orbits, resolving into a predictable orbit only when we observe it. At the point of our consciousness entering into seeing the path of the electron, it materializes solidly in this reality. Called forth by our interaction with it, the electron "chooses" from a realm of infinite possibilities the probability orbit that we limit it to by our observation. In other words, it goes from seemingly unpredictable wave-like behavior to a particle representation of reality when we see it that way. So, we really do not know what the electron is doing when we are not looking at it.

Do you see how important your observation is? When consciousness enters into this equation, it is said to collapse the wave (or more correctly, to collapse the wave function). At the subatomic level, it has been repeatedly proven that you cannot simultaneously observe a particle's momentum, or speed, and its position. If you fix one quality by measuring it, you always lose track of its corollary. In one experiment performed a few years ago, scientists slowed down the speed of light in a super-cooled vacuum to thirty-seven miles per hour. When they did this, the location of the molecules that they were observing in this vacuum completely disappeared!

Applying Quantum Concepts to Everyday Life

So, keeping in mind the importance of the observer effect, here is what I tell someone who is introduced to the principles of Matrix Energetics for the first time.

You think that you are composed of physical solid material and your problems are physical as well. Not so. If we reduce you to your most basic fundamental structures, we would find that you are composed of an orderly hierarchy of components (as if you were a stereo). In one sense, your body doesn't even really exist in the way that you have been taught to see it. Let me explain what I mean by that statement.

The body is composed of organic structures. These structures are made up of systems such as the respiratory system, digestive system, genito-urinary system, and so on. These systems are formed from organs made up of various types of specialized tissues. The tissues are composed of different cell types classified by their morphology as well as their functions. The cells are made of carbon-based molecules, and molecules are composed of atoms.

Now, at this point our linear model of physicality starts to get into some trouble. The nucleus of the atom has two structural components known as the proton and the neutron. The electron circulates in probability orbits, as I explained earlier. It is thought that when scientists attempt to measure or observe the "actual" orbit, the act of making that measurement collapses all of the possibility waves into a probable orbit. This new orbit will now have a weighted probability occurrence, because the act of our observation has collapsed or limited all other possible outcomes.

Indeed, everything at the subatomic level is susceptible to the observer effect. If you follow this down to its smallest unit that we have discovered to date, you get the photon, which is the basic unit of light. Photons can exist either as particles or waves, as I have already stated, depending on the observer's influence. If the act of observation changes the form or behavior of what's being observed, then consciousness must be included as an active and vital element in this description. You could say that in a real sense, the physical elements that make up what we call the material world spring into existence when we observe them. Here's the bottom line at our base level as a physical being: We are composed of light and information, or consciousness.

To illustrate how this information would be relevant to you, let's look at a real-life example. A man from Canada came in for a one-time visit to see if I could help with his frozen shoulder. This is a very painful condition that tremendously restricts the movement of the affected shoulder and arm. Its clinical course is long and chronic. Surgery or physical therapies, when employed, often do not appear to be that helpful. In fact, you are likely to be sent to a pain management clinic for counseling on how to live with the pain. My results with these cases at that time were generally not very good. Then a breakthrough occurred during this man's appointment.

At the time that he saw me, the condition had been present for about six months without any improvement. After he informed me that no one had been able to help him, I thought, "And you expect your experience with me to be any different?" I struggled to reduce his pain or to get some improvement in his range of motion for over an hour, and had actually worked up a sweat. I didn't know it at the time, but I was firmly locked into what I now call "the problem-set." In order to play the problem-set game, you must see the problem, realize that everyone who has tried to make a difference with it has failed, access all of the times in your life when you have failed at anything, adjust that for inflation, and then get that feeling of non-resourcefulness and "own" it. Now of course, you are armed with the tools you need to go out and make a difference. Or are you?

Feeling like a whipped dog, I was about to concede defeat when I intuitively heard the sound of laughter. Though surely originating within my own mind, the source of this etheric laughter seemed to be bouncing off the walls of the room. A taunting voice seemed to emerge from it, saying, "Look how hard he is working! Why does he feel that he has to do that?" To which a second voice, seemingly situated in another corner of the room, replied, "It is because of his low self-esteem."

"Yes," the first voice answered in agreement, "he thinks it is because of the way he was treated when he was little." The second voice boomed laughingly, "Just imagine it not there!" "Huh?" I thought, and looked at my patient's frozen shoulder. Shocked by the strange events occurring around me, I stepped out of consensus problem-driven reality. I was "seeing" instead of just looking, as don Juan talked about in the Castaneda books, *and the frozen shoulder was gone!*

Fast-forward four years. Here I was with another man complaining of a frozen shoulder. I was running about twenty minutes behind that morning, and to add insult to his injury, I was feeling very light-hearted and playful, engaging my patients and office staff in laughter as this man sat in my waiting room, unhappy and obviously in physical pain.

Finally, he was shown into the treatment room and sat with a big scowl on his face as I breezed in through the door. Picking up his chart, I looked down at the information there and said, "I see here that you have a frozen left shoulder." He nodded in agreement. What happened next, he tells me, forever changed his view of what constitutes reality.

I smiled, shook his right hand, and while looking directly into his eyes I told him that his frozen shoulder was beginning to thaw to my warm personality. Not giving him time to think or respond, I followed this statement by saying that the term "shoulder" was merely a consensus reality definition for something that wasn't there now. Having said that, I immediately lifted up his previously immobilized and painful appendage, demonstrating for him that his condition was perplexing, but not in any way serious. He responded by doubling over, no doubt a little in shock, and proceeded to let loose uproarious tides of laughter. When he finally regained control of his senses he exclaimed to me, "I see why you are so happy! Who wouldn't want a job like this?"

You see, in the first example, I was coming from a framework of belief that implied that life was a struggle. I would have to work really hard to be able to help my client at all. We both expected me to fail to do anything useful. I perfectly "out-pictured" our collective beliefs and rules of engagement. (Out-picturing refers to making a picture in your mind's eye, investing it with emotional energy or charge, and then having the experience of this picture and its charge as a physical event.) The encounter turned into a fight, featuring me in the ring against his condition.

In the second example, I was convinced of the ultimate unreality of his condition and was able to enter into a "quantum-ized" realm. From that state, the frozen shoulder was only one possible configuration of the atoms, cells, electrons, photons, and so on that made up what we in consensus reality have chosen to call a shoulder. Now, if the shoulder is ultimately just a pattern of high-energy photons, then they can be reconfigured based on how we choose to observe them. That makes the problem a lot less daunting.

Just as we can be convinced that our reality and our diagnosis are correct (even though according to statistics compiled at the Mayo

Clinic, almost 50 percent of its diagnoses were proven on autopsy to be wrong, dead wrong!), we could choose to be equally convinced of the insubstantiality of the problem. I say this not to make light of people's suffering, but to point out that at another, equally real level of reality, the problem as well as the possible solution is light! Following the silly but sage advice of my "guides," I imagined it "not there," and it wasn't. What a difference the framework of your perceptions and beliefs can make.

Just recently, with the advent of the message board on the Matrix Energetics website, people have been telling me that they are learning how to do these things simply by reading about them and applying what is taught there. One chiropractor learned how to apply the concepts of "Two-Point" and "Time Travel" just by seeing me demonstrate them on the streaming video posted on the website. This doctor wrote of his experience on the message board, describing an encounter with a patient who came into his office for help with a broken toe. He did what the video example showed, conceptually Time Traveling her toe back to before it had been broken, and suddenly the bone moved under his hand as he held her foot, "Two-Pointing" the injury. Two minutes later, she walked out of his office, no longer in pain and with no limp.

A woman who thought that what I said about Time Travel made a lot of sense and sounded doable left another message. Experimenting with it, she undoubtedly accessed the morphic field for Matrix Energetics, and experienced the following result. She writes:

Hi. After reading on this website some of the information about counting backwards (Time Travel) I tried it, and was able to go back to a time before I was four years old. Our family moved out of state, away from the relatives that nurtured and loved me, and since then I have not been able to experience nurturing and loving at all. Finally, last night I could remember what nurturing feels like, for the first time in my life since that age. I am a recycled teenager now. Now I can feel my heart chakra beginning to open. All of this has happened since I visited the website and heard Richard on Contact Talk Radio this Wednesday.

Messages like this are just like words from heaven to me. Experiences like these offer confirmation that I am following what Buddhist philosophy calls "right livelihood."

Even though I am the proud holder of two medical degrees, I have just about dropped out of the medical mode in my office. If you think about it, a doctor is someone you pay to observe you as having problems. In fact, a doctor's job, and rightly so, is to rule out the diseases or conditions that are most life-threatening based on your symptoms and clinical findings. It is an awful but sometimes necessary job. The physician must dwell in a reality where he is constantly on guard and thinking of the worst things that could happen to his patients—after all, you wouldn't want him to miss anything. In conventional medicine, it is apparently better to engage in overkill for diagnosis. I was told in medical school that if a man over forty came in with pain anywhere between his nose and his penis you must first rule out a heart attack!

I am not saying that diagnosis and treatment are not necessary. They define what we consider the existing paradigm for health care in this country. I am grateful that medical science has been elevated to such a level of precision and knowledge. But there are so many good doctors out there; maybe I don't have to occupy all of my time and energy laboring to do what so many already do exceptionally well.

I look at this issue from the perspective of music—my first love. You would not expect James Taylor to play or sound like Jimi Hendrix. They are two unique identities who interpreted music through their own hearts and awareness. What if there were a standard for musicians, like there is for medical doctors, where they would all have to be able to play and perform just like Jimi (or James) because that was the accepted standard of musical care?

That is one of the reasons I chose Chiropractic and Naturopathic medical degrees, because these professions still embrace the eclectic spirit. While it is wonderful that the science of medicine has grown to such great maturity, let us never forget or abandon the Art of medicine. The necessary counterpart of dry mechanical knowledge and procedures must always reside within the heart and soul of the healer. This is something that one just is; it cannot be taught in medical school as an elective course.

In Matrix Energetics we choose a different path from the reliance on ideas that embrace a diagnosis-and-treatment model of health care. We hold a state of awareness and enter into a kind of energetic rapport with clients, holding for them what the shamanic cultures would call "sacred space" so that they can have the freedom to choose to express a different outcome. Often, the trouble is that no one ever tells you with any real sense of conviction that you have that choice.

So ultimately, you are the one, with a lot of help, who makes up the rules for your experience of this reality. Wouldn't it be great if you noticed that your version of the rules for your reality wasn't working so well, and you could exercise your freedom to choose to release some of your negative or limiting beliefs and concepts? If something is not working for you and you realize that it is possibly within your power to change it, wouldn't you be willing to try to make your outcomes a better match for your deep desires? This reminds me of something one of my inner guides once told me: a different take on a phrase from the Serenity Prayer. My guide's version was, "God give me the grace to accept the things that I cannot change. And grant unto me the power to change the things that I cannot accept!"

Remember the example of what I did with the man's frozen shoulder earlier in this chapter? I chose to observe it differently, playfully deconstructing each element of his experience of the problem that was overwhelming to him. First I told him, "It's not frozen, it's beginning to thaw in the presence of my warm personality." Second, I informed him that it was not a shoulder. In the reality I chose to sustain, his shoulder was one small part of the wavefront of consciousness and virtual particles of which he is composed. Finally, getting in tune with the state of quantum possibility, I slipped my awareness into a realm where his shoulder did not exist as a problem. Since I chose with great conviction a state of possibility where the perfect outcome could manifest, actual transformation of the physical matter hologram of his shoulder was achieved.

I have a contention, more like a strong suspicion, that physicists just make up a lot of stuff about virtual particles. We have beautiful mathematical equations to describe them, but no one has ever seen one, since they are too small. We have measured them indirectly by how their presence changes or deforms the environment that they are indirectly measured in.

Maybe this is like when we get a cold. We do not actually ever see the virus, and in fact, the cold does not directly cause our symptoms. They are caused by the reactions within our body's internal environment when our immune system responds to the invading germ or bug. We never directly experience the cold. We really experience our body's attempt to kill the virus; and for the most part, this is the source of our symptoms. Perhaps in some way the quantum physicists' virtual particles are the bug in our reality, but our consciousness responding to them is really what we notice as our experience of reality.

Physicists theorize that because virtual particles are so small and usually only exist within infinitesimally small periods of time, unlimited energy can be contained within the space of their existence. In order to get some idea of what this experiment might mean in real terms, just think about the power we unleashed when we split the atom. In the blink of an eye, there could be a whole universe that springs into being and dies or dissolves. Because we cannot measure it, the rules are not broken for what is physically possible. But as soon as we see it, we must observe it obeying the rules that we think it should.

You contain within you the keys to inestimable power and limitless possibility as long as you do not actually try to make anything happen. Whenever you relinquish the tendency to measure or observe with your conscious limitations, since you are composed of quantum stuff, anything is theoretically possible. You can tell me that my conclusions are wrong, but consider the bumblebee; scientists say that aerodynamically it should not be able to fly, but it does not know this "fact," so it continues to fly anyway. Just so, I am content to bumble along entertaining the consciousness of an infinite realm of miraculous possibility, largely because I don't know that I can't!

4

A Scientific Shift in Reality

Y OU DON'T HAVE TO BE EINSTEIN TO DO THIS. In addition, I don't want anyone reading this book to think that in order to do what I teach in the "right" way, they have to become carbon copies of me. I don't want people to think, "Well Richard said . . . and so that must be right." Keep in mind that Richard doesn't know. Just because you can do something and make it reproducible and reliable, that doesn't mean you understand it; I get in my car and drive to work every day, but I actually have no idea how the internal piston mechanism or any of the other technical stuff works. But I can drive with reasonable competence and without thinking about it too much.

Just because quantum physicists have detailed all of these pretty mathematical equations about virtual particles and wave mechanics, this doesn't guarantee that they really understand the inner workings of our mysterious and magical universe. So do not for one moment imagine that you have to completely understand the principles of everything that I share with you in these pages. I am actually making a lot of it up, as are the physicists. As long as we share a powerful and congruent reality, it will still work for you, perhaps even better than it does for me. Remember also that it was Einstein who said that imagination is more important than knowledge, and many people have called him the smartest man who ever lived.

What I really want you to deeply understand now is that if your head is full of ideas about the way you thought everything must be, it might not be that way at all. In fact, if your head is empty of all of that complexity—the folds and undulations of thoughts and gray matter—it might be better able to understand what I am conveying to you now. What might be more useful here is the ability to adapt to a new way of thinking.

Spirit and Science

Descartes put forth some of the key concepts that became identified with the philosophy of the Western mind-set. Indeed, Descartes' ideas have been influential in the formation of the field of medicine. He put forth the notion that the makeup of man, at least physically, could be compared to that of a well-made clock. From this viewpoint a healthy man was a functioning clock, and a sick or diseased person was like a broken clock. You can see within the context of this statement the founding rationale for the philosophical approach of modern medicine.

Religious doctrine at the time of the Renaissance also wanted to keep control of matters of the Spirit, and didn't want scientists rearranging the framework of its beliefs. This caused some problems for one great astronomer, Galileo, who identified the primary qualities of matter, and consequently reinforced the division between science and spirit. Galileo was trying to say that the earth was not the center of the universe. If scientific speculation was seen as heresy by the church authorities, their response was to pressure the unfortunate scientist into recanting his statements.

To keep from falling into disfavor, and coincidentally to save his own skin, Galileo defined the primary qualities of matter as things that could be observed and measured. Wisely, he did not attempt to comment on secondary qualities of matter, deeming these things to be the intellectual and moral terrain of the church and of royalty. By defining things in this manner, Galileo hoped to avoid taking controversial stances that could get him into trouble—or perhaps even killed for his efforts. So this is where the split between what was considered spiritual or intangible and the "real" material world began.

This approach to how reality is defined makes us, in a sense, fragmented in our awareness, splitting emotion and faith from the so-called hard sciences, so that we begin to question and disbelieve anything that cannot be proven to us by hard evidence and physical findings of fact. It is with the marginalization of those experiences that are outside what can be proven and demonstrated scientifically that we begin to die a little inside to the world of spirit, the territorial realm of the shaman and the wise woman.

Models of Reality in Classical Newtonian Physics

According to Newtonian thinking, in a closed system there are a finite number of forces. If you add those forces together while understanding the basic laws that govern their particle-based interactions, you should ultimately be able to predict and analyze everything in the known universe. In classical physics we live in a material world. All things in nature are made up of and result from the sum of their parts, and are constructed of physical particles. There is no animating intelligence or vital life force that inhabits these particles.

Everything can be understood because it can be divisible into its parts, and all things obey set laws both on Earth and in the cosmos. There is stability and dependability in a world constructed in this manner. This reductionist scientific vision is perfectly illustrated in a segment of the *Cosmos* television series in which Carl Sagan stirs a giant cauldron of molecules and wonders why they still have not created life.

Science Is Still Attempting to "Get It Right"

Because the scientific approach is so fragmented, science has to continually revise its theories to account for variables that were missed the first time. Each succeeding attempt to describe the laws of physical existence requires a new mathematical formula. Then, when some enterprising scientist performs an experiment and the results fail to gel with the established concepts of what scientists until that point have believed to be true and proven about the way things work, a new premise arises.

When these new experimental results are reproduced even in the face of what has been assumed to be true up to that point, then a new theory or equation must be developed that mathematically explains, or at least offers a theoretical framework from which to explain, how the new "contradictory" finding can actually be correct. If the math that has been developed provides a theoretical basis for explaining the puzzling lab data, then after many experiments have been performed confirming the new hypothesis, the theory is assumed to be correct, at least for the specifics related to the phenomena that it is describing. But just because the math equations work out does not mean that we've really got an accurate description of how the world works.

Einstein Reintroduces Imagination

I could say that Einstein's theories were pretty crazy, but his belief in imagination did a great service to the discipline of science. In order to develop the ideas and concepts for his famous theory of relativity, Einstein performed what he called "thought experiments." In one such experiment, he visualized what it would be like to ride a beam of light, imagining what it would look like as he sped past a stationary object at such a speed. This sounds crazy, but it is the experiment he performed in his imagination, which he then back-engineered mathematically into a series of equations that would come to be known as the theory of relativity. The important thing to note here is that he had the experience, or the journey, to use a shamanic term, and then he created the equation that explained what he had found out from his inner experience; he made it up.

This is not at all an isolated example. Many great scientific discoveries have occurred as the result of a visionary experience or the flash of an intuitive insight. Consider the inventor and scientist Nikola Tesla. Tesla's father was sure that his son would follow in his footsteps by taking over the family business some day, but the universal design had a greater plan for young Nikola. One day he became very ill with a high fever that nearly devastated him, and he was not expected to survive. Nikola said to his father that if by some chance he survived, he would not take over the family business, but would instead go to school to become an engineer. Tesla dreamed of one day harnessing the tremendous power of Niagara Falls by converting it into usable electrical energy. Indeed, one of the many things that he invented was something now called a Tesla coil. This coil allowed for the conversion of energy derived from rushing water, via a water-powered turbine, into electrical power. The power was then stored for use as needed.

Tesla did survive his illness and went on to engineering school, eventually ending up in the employment of Thomas Edison. One day, while feeding pigeons in the park at twilight, Tesla had a vision of a vast, oscillating universe that was made up of frequencies of energy. He developed one of these frequencies that he experienced in this mystical state, harnessing the one that vibrated at sixty cycles per second—which might sound familiar to you. It should, because that is the frequency for electric alternating current. Even though Edison's name and his company, General Electric, are typically associated with electricity, it was actually Tesla who harnessed alternating current to power our world.

Another famous example of how a dream or vision became translated into a scientific breakthrough is the discovery of the structure of the benzene ring, by German chemist F. A. Kekulé. In Kekulé's own words:

> I turned my chair towards the fireplace and sank into a doze. Again, the atoms that I had been pondering about were flitting before my eyes. Smaller groups now kept modestly in the background. My mind's eye, sharpened by repeated visions of a similar sort, now distinguished larger structures of varying forms. Long rows frequently rose together, all in movement, winding and turning like serpents: and see! What was that? One of the serpents seized its own tail and the form whirled mockingly before my eyes. I came awake like a flash of lightning. This time I spent the remainder of the night working out the consequences of the hypothesis.

In other words, he entered an altered state, viewed an answer to what had been puzzling him, and upon returning to waking consensus reality spent the rest of the night making his chemical structure or equation conform to his flash of intuitive insight. He made it up! Many of the scientific discoveries and theories that we now consider to comprise the bedrock of scientific thought are the result of the dreams, visions, or altered states of geniuses who could access the right-brain or subconscious mind.

But even geniuses are susceptible to consensus reality. As wonderful as Einstein's leaps into imagination were, for example, he was still reticent to let go of certain concepts of reality. Einstein himself did not like the direction in which his theories of relativity and the space-time continuum were pointing. Although he contributed some breakthrough concepts, he resisted the idea of relinquishing his classical physics paradigm in order to examine the postulations of the emerging branch of physics that would come to be known as quantum mechanics. With the advent of Einstein's relativity theory, the paradigm of classical physics was only slightly modified in order to account for his observations concerning moving frames of reference.

With Einstein's equations came the idea that the physical parameters of the electron could be different depending on the methodology that was chosen to observe them. The idea of a solid, particle-based universe was still not in question at all.

Quantum Physics and Weird Reality

With the formulation of the theories of quantum physics, reality was to a certain extent redefined, and the rules changed when dealing with things the size of an electron or smaller. At the level of the quantum, the perception of what makes up what we call reality was determined to be experiencer-dependent. Reality, to some extent at this level of energy, could be said to be relative to the eye of the beholder. Quantum theory yielded consistent mathematical models that could be used to experimentally predict the behavior of particles and energy states at the level of virtual particles and photons.

However, I hasten to add that just because these models appear to predict the behavior of subatomic particles, quantum physics theory is still unable to explain some of the basic paradoxes that have puzzled physicists since the time of Newton. For example, gravity still does not fit into the model anywhere, and for some time now Super String Theory has attempted to explain and integrate the forces of nature into one unified field theory, which to this day eludes explanation. Remember what I have been saying here; just because it makes mathematical sense, and we have pretty equations to describe life at the quantum level of existence, this still does not mean that the theories are correct. They are simply the best guesstimate we can arrive at, for the moment.

What I'd like you to notice about these scientists is that "facts" are not so cut and dried as hypothesis-experiments. There is a lot of play and imagination, and a lot of insight and inspiration. The scientists are just "making it up." In fact, the word "fact" comes from the Latin, factum, which means "made up." So it is great to believe in science if it offers you a view of reality that is useful, but if it does not, then I want you to feel free to recreate your reality with your imagination and insight. If it is more useful to you, then it doesn't matter what science says, since the scientists seem to be making it up anyway.

Math as Mysticism

Mathematics in its higher forms is a highly abstract language that pays homage more to the realm of the artist or the dreamer than it represents the cold, hard realm of scientific fact. The ability to dream, or to enter and harvest ideas from altered states, is a crucial skill that many genius scientists and inventors have exhibited in a highly developed form. Remember that if we base our assessments of what is real only on what others have demonstrated, which has become dogma and accepted fact, then we will simply prove only what our predecessors imagined was possible. We will not discover any new scientific territory.

We need to do what the queen said in *Alice's Adventures in Wonderland*: We need to "believe as many as six impossible things before breakfast." If we do this as a daily habit we will begin to have experiences and thoughts that do not merely maintain the orthodox party line of normal, consensual reality. Instead, we will begin to inhabit within the domain of our thoughts a realm of wondrous and magical possibility. It is from such a realm that the experience of Matrix Energetics originates and resides.

So when scientists have transformative visions, they must then take those visions and translate them into the language of mathematics. Other scientists may then study their theories and come to some sort of agreement about their viability as scientific postulates. But in so doing, there is always the chance that something can become obscured or lost in translation.

Even with brilliant insights and dreams, there are always those pieces that never quite fit. What do we do with those? You have to develop some other mathematical language that addresses the special circumstances or phenomena that do not quite conform to the literal interpretation and math of the theory—for example, that pesky force of gravity. Einstein, like so many others, was looking for that Holy Grail of science: the Unified Field Theory. He had to invent the theory of general relativity to address the gravity problem, and at the end of his life he was still looking for a way to fit all of the pieces together into a single, all-encompassing theory. According to his own published comments, he failed to accomplish this goal.

So maybe gravity is something we just made up to explain other things that we couldn't understand. What if all of our scientific theories have fatal flaws in them and we simply cannot see where the flaws are? What if somewhere in our exposition of the laws of physics we screwed up? Instead of grasping a very simple truth, maybe we opted for a complex explanation with lots of math and everyone accepted it as true because all of the numbers seemed to add up. Have we made the mistake of equating mathematical precision and impressive theories with an actual description of the physical properties of our universe?

How could our assumptions be wrong when they can so precisely predict the outcome of physical forces and phenomena? Consider for a moment that our science still harkens back to Descartes and Galileo. If we cannot explain something, then we will not talk about it; we will even proceed to invent mathematical equations without taking into account the piece that is giving us trouble. ESP is one example that comes to mind. It has been studied for a century or more, and at one point in our history was even developed and taught as a reproducible ability that could be utilized to gather military intelligence in the Remote Viewers Stargate program. Do not think for one moment that the military would have studied this if they could not produce credible data about its use with precision and clarity.

Yet, whenever you talk about ESP or strange feats of the mind someone always trots out the Amazing Randi, whose sole talent seems to be unrelenting skepticism to the point of virtual blindness. If it is not in his paradigm it cannot exist, and therefore must be a clever trick or simply a delusion. Randi has offered a million-dollar reward to anyone who can successfully prove the existence of the supernatural: something beyond the evidence of his five senses. What are Randi's criteria, you might ask? If he doesn't accept that you have demonstrated something that he cannot explain, then it doesn't exist. To date, no one has claimed the prize. Do you think Randi is highly motivated to discover something outside his belief parameters? I'd give a million-to-one odds against that!

I think our scientists also operate within the framework of philosophical blinders. Can you imagine a theory of everything that goes against the accepted conventional theories of Newton and Einstein? Even if a scientist's logic and equations could impeccably demonstrate that the theory of relativity was flawed, or worse, just plain wrong, do you think many people would be inclined to listen, much less believe? How much does unconscious peer pressure serve to dictate what we are willing to accept as possible if it goes against established scientific tradition and the pillars of Western logic?

I like to believe that if something happens once and is reproducible, then there is probably a law operating within the framework of that manifestation. Because it is outside of our daily expectations to be able to experience a miracle, I think our conscious minds edit the information and energy that might allow us to recall those types of experiences at will.

Of course, there is another way to go about the art and practice of manifesting the things you want in your life. The best explanations are often those that on the surface appear to be the simplest. At the risk of offending the more skeptical or scientifically minded reader, I will share with you an equation for this state of mind. Are you ready? All right then, here it is: "Let go and let God."

When I hit that bridge at sixty-five miles per hour, I did not have time for a long and complicated prayer. Instead, my prayer was "Michael," as in the Archangel of protection, and "Shit," which if I had time for one last act in this life, is probably what I would have done! The response was instantaneous and miraculous. One very wise spiritual teacher whom I have had the pleasure to know said, "Pray as if everything depends on the Angels or God. Act as if everything depends on you!" At that moment, no further action could be taken, so I let go and put my all into one last powerful plea—and I am still here to share these things with you.

The point is that you want to entertain in your imagination, as well as in the substance of your beliefs, the ability to create and sustain states that are more powerful than you in your limited conscious awareness. Even if you only believe you are making it up, do it really well so that you have more options than are accessible in your normal waking state. It's even better to set up the parameters of your manifestation in such a way that things get taken care of before a crisis arises.

Observing Light Particles with a Quantum Lens

Scientists discovered that light could exhibit the qualities of either a particle or a wave. In a classic experiment by British physicist Thomas Young in the early 1800s, an electron beam the width of a single electron was shot at a wall across the room with two slits in it. When one slit or the other was covered up, the electrons would hit the wall after passing through the single slit and register an imprint on the photographic plate. The distribution of the pattern suggested that the electron was behaving like a particle.

If both slots were then uncovered and the electron beam was again shot toward the wall, the single electron appeared to somehow split and go through both slits simultaneously. This created an interference pattern on the film that looked like white and then dark horizontal lines. This pattern was similar to what you might expect when a series of waves are added together.

Sometimes the resulting pattern would create a greater image on the wall and sometimes the "waves" of electrons appeared to cancel each other out, creating an interference pattern that was seen to be smaller or less dense than what was expected from the sum of the wave patterns. What was really weird about this was that when the paths of the electrons shot from the beam were measured or observed, the pattern that resulted exhibited a distribution on the photographic plate that would be expected from a particle. But, when no one was looking or measuring, it produced patterns that were wave-like. *So, the inescapable conclusion was that at the level of the world of the electron or photon, the act of observing the electron's path caused it to behave differently than it did when no one was "watching" it. For this reason, the physical character of light was said to be observer-dependent.*

You are composed of electrons, which can and do behave differently depending on the observer's perspective or set of expectations. Knowing this, you can begin to understand how a physical pattern or condition could change if you chose to congruently observe that condition or problem from a quantum perspective: what I have chosen to call "wavefront consciousness."

I discuss principles of quantum physics so that you can learn to embrace some key concepts that fall outside of your everyday expectations. If you think what you are learning is a bit weird, you are in good company with the thoughts and theorems of some of the most brilliant scientists the world has ever known. One of my students told me she was a little apprehensive about telling her son, a physics major, what she would be learning in my seminar because he had always expressed disdain for "woo-woo" subjects. After looking over the materials describing the seminar's contents, he said to his mother, "This is the least woo-woo thing that you have done; everything that they are talking about is, at least in theory, covered in my graduate-level physics classes. This stuff has a scientific basis, Mom."

5

Learning to Engage a Solution-Set

YOU ARE WHAT YOU THINK. Everything that you have believed, accepted, experienced, and internalized comprises a vast matrix or grid that defines what I call your energetic signature. What you have learned forms the perceptual lens you use to subconsciously filter all of the information in your worldview. Your experience of your five senses makes up what you think of as your reality. In order to change something in that perceived reality territory, you must alter or change the arrangement of your thoughts and feelings. Trying to fit new knowledge into what you already think you know is not the best way to make a paradigmatic shift. I always assume that I don't really "know" anything, which opens me to pay attention to what I might learn in the next moment.

Shifting the Matrix of Reality Through the Use of Questions

I like to ask myself a few key questions in the morning as part of a ritual that sets the state for my day. "What haven't I thought of yet? What can I discover that will serve to confuse as well as enlighten me a little more today?" If you want to change your experience of your daily reality fare, come as you are, but finish your day having learned something new. Questions are one of the ways to do this consistently and elegantly. *When you start to habitually ask open-ended questions of the universe, it starts to answer back, teaching you new things.*

When you change the way you observe and encode your reality, you are in effect changing the consciousness structure of what you choose to observe. You are becoming a co-creator in this new reality template that you have begun to experience. By loosening up your old way of looking, you begin to actually see into and live this new domain. When you do this consistently, with a feeling of internal conviction and resolve, your experience of the so-called physical world and all of its preconditioning will begin to morph and change. In some cultures, this process describes the way of the Shaman, or Warrior of the Spirit.

Matrix Energetics Represents a Way to Transform Your Experience of Reality

Einstein said that you can't do the same thing in the same way and expect to get a different result. You have to go outside that linear pattern of habitual thinking and have a new thought, which you then apply to your perception of reality in order to get a different outcome. You have to paint outside the lines, or go outside the box. Matrix Energetics is my attempt to make sense of the day Superman appeared in my office. Over time, his appearance transformed my entire concept of what reality actually is.

Once I had been so transformed, I began to ask new types of questions of myself, and to order my perceptions and thought patterns in a new way. Then I had to make sense of the experiences that I was now having, and put into place some kind of philosophy or worldview that would be congruent with the experiences of my new state.

Be Careful How You Frame Questions

If good questions can open new possibilities and transform your world, the same is true for negatively focused questions. Over time, you set up grids of energy in your subconscious awareness. These habitual patterns become the templates from which you manifest changes and events in your physical world. If you put enough mental and emotional energy into manifesting the things that you habitually worry about, you eventually manifest physically the fruit of your negative expectations and beliefs. Perhaps this is one reason why Job says in the Bible (and I paraphrase), "The thing which I have feared has come upon me." One of our first tasks is to short-circuit this typical approach to medical problems, conditions, and even reality itself. By changing your reality template you begin to build a platform for new experiences of altered states.

Things Don't Always Have to Be What They Seem

This reminds me of a fairly dramatic example of how devastating a limiting belief can be in an unusual situation. One evening, Mark Dunn and I had returned to the office after a weekend seminar. As we stood there talking, I got an idea that I wanted to muscle-test. With typical "bull in the china shop" enthusiasm, I charged ahead, quickly coming up with an off-the-cuff and spur-of-the-moment testing protocol. I had Mark hold out his arm so that I could muscle-test him for a product line we wanted to incorporate into our clinical toolbox. I got a weak muscle response when testing him as he held the product. This signified that his body was cooperating with the focus of our intent.

Anchoring Devices

We had done this kind of investigative work together frequently, making use of what is called in the field of Neuro-Linguistic Programming and behavioral psychology an "anchor." Once you have learned a new behavior, you can then internalize and streamline it so that the desired response is triggered whenever you activate a specific unique sensory stimulus (the anchor). Using such a consciousness strategy, you can readily enter into any state that you have visited many times before.

Once you cross that consciousness threshold, your perceptional filters can become highly altered at will. This is exactly what happened to both of us as we fully entered into the experimenter's mind-set. Ready for just about anything, our senses and perceptions were in a heightened awareness—the result of many such sessions.

A good example of what I am referring to here is the trance state that will eventually result with repeated listening to a CD or live performance of Shamanic drumming. This form of repetitive drumming distracts the conscious mind, lulling the left brain into relinquishing for a time its stranglehold over the prevailing view of reality. After much practice, right-brain hemispheric dominance temporarily occurs and the process Jung called "active imagination" is allowed free rein. In Shamanic lore, this is called a journey. In these journeys, you may encounter mindscapes of a virtual territory of specifically identified terrains, which have been mapped out by consciousness explorers of many cultures for thousands of years.

It is as if these inner realities are like some cosmic video game with discrete levels and sections. You can create a virtual doorway into these other realms if you are willing to spend the time and energy to develop the necessary trance state. I believe that anyone with sufficient practice and motivation can learn to enter these non-ordinary realities or mindscapes. The same can be said about Matrix Energetics. Anyone can learn the techniques of Matrix Energetics and enter into specific, sustained states of altered awareness. It is in this realm that magic and physics meet to form a tenuous partnership.

What I am about to relate to you is merely one page in the book that I have come to refer to as "The Misadventures of Mark." I had just muscle-tested him for the product that he was holding. Performing an activity we had done thousands of times previously, I lightly tapped on the top of his head at a specific acupuncture point. My intent for this activity was to "tell" the brain to put this information on display. I imagine this to be like projecting the image of a three-dimensional hologram into the space in front of you. In the special rule set that I made up for this procedure, the act of tapping instructs the brain to hold the desired information at the forefront of one's consciousness so that it might be preferentially seen and acted upon.

What happened next was highly dramatic, if not wholly unexpected, given some of my partner's misadventures from past clinical experiments gone wrong. Suddenly, Mark's eyes closed and he fell back against the wall. He proceeded to slide down the wall, then slumped forward unceremoniously onto the floor. Completely unable to move and nearly unconscious, he lay there like a slain lamb in some sort of tale of sacrifice to angry gods. I am somewhat used to this kind of behavior from him, so I was not unduly alarmed; it was just the rapidity of this particular episode of "tales of the unconscious" that caught me a little off guard.

No stranger to altered states, with a sigh I realized that once again I would have to follow the hare where the hounds would not venture. Feeling somewhat responsible, I dropped into an altered brainwave pattern I had learned in some of the meditative and shamanic exercises I have dabbled in. As soon as I closed my eyes, I found myself standing on a cliff high above a beach. Looking down far below, I saw that someone's body had apparently been dashed upon the rocks. I will give you three guesses whose it was. "Uh-oh," I thought. "That cannot possibly be good."

Looking above me, I saw something that looked a little like the tail of an enormous kite floating high in the wind. Resolved to do whatever it would take to bring back my friend's wayward soul essence, I leapt up into the sky. Aiming high above, I engaged in rapid pursuit of the object, which was flipping and twisting in the wind. I reached out and lunged forward, getting a firm grip on Mark's soul essence. "Got you." Quickly, I willed us to return back to our bodies, which were sitting semi-unoccupied on the floor of the office.

Opening my eyes, I mimicked what I had seen my shamanic practitioner friend do. I stuffed the essence, which I still held tightly in my ephemeral/etheric hand, back into Mark's chest. Moments later he slowly opened his eyes, coming back to our mutually shared consensus reality. One small problem remained to be solved. He still was, for all intents and purposes, totally paralyzed. This sort of outcome to our consciousness experiments had occurred before, and Mark came out of those times relatively unscathed. In truth, I was not too concerned about his current predicament. We'd both "been there, done that."

As he lay there, mentally mapping the state and condition of his bodily functions, he said something that momentarily chilled me to the bone. Mark said, "I am fine with this really, but what if nothing like this had ever happened to me and I woke up some morning in my bed like this? I probably would believe that I had a stroke and buy into that reality. Conceivably, I could remain like this for the rest of my life." Now that is a scary thought!

I do not mean to imply here that strokes are merely an experience of an altered perceptual reality, and that all you have to do is wake up from the dream into some other parallel world. Sometimes, having no ready reference point for a new experience, someone might take my statements at face value only. That is not my intent here at all. It is just an interesting possibility that I believe is worth considering. If you never entertain in your mind the possibility of a different outcome or explanation, no other possibility can arise in your thinking and thus in your experience of the world. In the Copenhagen interpretation of quantum physics, there is nothing inside the box until you look in it. Your act of observation somehow creates the version of reality that you observe. If that isn't an example of thinking outside the box, then nothing is.

For the next ten minutes Mark and I did what we do so well. We played with the situation of his holographic paralysis until we found a possibility state that did not encode for that peculiar outcome. After a little tweaking Mark could stand up and walk, but his body was still out-picturing some disturbing body language. He no longer appeared to be paralyzed—an obvious improvement. He now resembled an adult male who had grown up with cerebral palsy, with perhaps a few echoes of the stroke pattern still playing itself out in his neurology. Probing the depths of alternate scenarios and playing this deeply are very taxing, so we decided we needed to eat. You should have seen the looks on people's faces in their cars as we walked the short half block to our favorite restaurant. Mark looked a little like a demented version of Igor in the *Frankenstein* Hollywood mythology, with his right arm frozen across his body, forearm held rigidly across his chest. I watched him slide his foot along the gravel like a strange parody of Boris Karloff's stride in the movie *The Mummy's Tomb*. Thank God this had happened to him before with no apparent long-term effects, or I might have been really concerned.

When we sat down to eat, the owner waved and smiled at us as if there were nothing out of the ordinary. (My take on this was that familiarity really does breed *content*.) We finished dinner and slowly trekked back to the office, where Mark started to get a little bit agitated. He stubbornly insisted that this had been fun, but he now had to go to a party where he was expected to put in an appearance. I told him that he was a little bit crazy if he expected to be able to drive in his current physical condition. "Besides," I said, "if you did somehow manage to safely drive there, they would call 911 when they got a look at you!" Reluctantly, he agreed that this made sense, so I folded him into my car and headed for home. He just needed to sleep off the effects and would undoubtedly be right as rain: a metaphor that particularly holds water in a city like Seattle.

When we arrived at my house my wife took one look at Mark's condition and stated matter-of-factly, "You boys have been playing with energy again, I see." That said, she turned smartly on her heel and bustled off to the spare bedroom to turn down the sheets for our hapless guest. With an expression of resigned and good-natured exhaustion, Mark threw himself on the bed and was soon fast asleep. The next morning when I came downstairs for breakfast, I found him already at the kitchen table, fully recovered and apparently no worse for wear. He laughed when I sat down at the table. "Let's not go there ever again," he said. Just another ordinary day at the office!

I believe that the concepts and practices of our Western medicine system have taken on an importance in our subconscious mind-set equal to that of a mythology. Anything so ingrained into our awareness becomes part of the foundation of our reality. In order to change the expected outcomes in health or disease, you have to move outside the prefabricated box that is ensouled by that set of expectations. To achieve a new or different outcome, you must move into a state of non-consensus reality where the rules of the game may not be so rigidly defined. *Try playing by a different set of rules, or go to a different game entirely. A new game enables you to be free enough to produce congruent, objective changes in every aspect of your life.* Taking full responsibility for what you create allows you to make up the rules as you go along.

Miracle Mind-Sets

I am currently fascinated with someone by the name of John of God. This man, who has no formal medical education, goes into trance and incorporates the consciousness of some long-deceased surgeon, who then takes over John's consciousness completely. John of God's personality is submerged into the subconscious background, and the entity, which obviously has finely-honed surgical skills, takes over and performs the surgeries, often with only a dull scalpel. The patients are also in a trance state, and no anesthesia or medications are used. This takes place in a small village in Brazil, and people flock there daily for treatments. Two visible surgeries are performed each day so that people can see a representation of what is possible in an environment and consciousness that has been dedicated and consecrated for many years through continual prayer and meditation. In fact, there are as many as fifty spirit mediums who remain in deep meditation throughout the course of the operations and activities each day.

This has been going on since John of God was sixteen years old. Imagine the dedication and perseverance of this undoubtedly holy man, who has given over his entire life in service to God for the sole purpose of alleviating the suffering of his fellow man. Imagine, for a moment, the reality of his life. He wakes up, bathes, eats breakfast, and then goes to the area where sometimes as many as a thousand supplicants wait for him. He arrives at the chapel, joining in the prayers of the faithful. Then he slips into deep trance, takes a sudden breath as a change overcomes his countenance, and just that smoothly, the consciousness of the spirit surgeon arrives. Without hesitation, the operating intelligence, if you pardon the small pun, washes his hands, picks up the surgical instrument of choice that is held out to him by an assistant, and with no further ado, he turns to the waiting patient—who is also in a deep trance—and begins the indicated operation.

In the video of John of God I saw, he sliced open a woman's abdomen and then without any sign of hesitation or trepidation, he plunged his bare fingers deep into the surgical wound, rooting around in the exposed abdominal tissue for something, which apparently was removed to the satisfaction of the operating intelligence. Then the spirit doctor, again with hands that have obviously expertly performed this feat thousands of times, stitched up the wound with needle and thread, completing the procedure. All the while, the patient remained in a state of deep trance, never moving and with no visible signs of any discomfort. If you want evidence of what is possible from within a profoundly altered state of consciousness, then you need look no further.

Now, I am quite a bit more selfish than this man, and in no way could currently aspire to the saintly level of conduct that his degree of dedication demonstrates. Imagine what it would be like to wake up in the morning, go into a trance and completely lose conscious awareness of your surroundings, and then come to at the end of the day, unaware of anything that you have done in the course of it. Talk about an example of your basic self-sacrificing service! Thank goodness that level of saintly dedication is not necessary to successfully do Matrix Energetics, because if it were, it most certainly would not be me who would be talking to you now. Saint Richard? I think not.

But there is a novel idea that can be derived from this example. If you are largely unconscious of the healings that have occurred in the course of a day, that means your conscious mind, the part of you that makes judgments about what is or is not possible, cannot screw up your access and appreciation for that state of being that I often refer to as a state of grace, or the Miracle mind-set. When I contemplate the act of performing feats such as I have just described, I cannot even consciously comprehend it as a reality for me. This is not to imply that I am ruling such things out, because I would never close the door on the appearance of the miraculous and the unexpected in my life. Remember, the Bible tells us that we often entertain Angels unawares. By opening our minds to the possibility that such things are possible, we entertain at the subconscious level the state of mind that is the open door to the realm of seemingly miraculous manifestations.

One of the best ways that we can aspire to perform any task or to meet any goal currently beyond our conscious grasp is to model the state and abilities of someone else who is already able to do the thing that we want to experience and ultimately master. Our current perceptions about what is possible have been shamelessly inculcated, conforming to the medical model of health and disease currently in power in our Western civilization. I believe that the reason we do not really see anyone like John of God in this country is that our accepted cultural model molds the very energy of consciousness, the morphic field, and as a result we produce only the manifestations and outcomes that are in line with the dictates of our subconscious beliefs and expectations.

Brazil, like the Philippines, is predominantly Catholic. The people of these countries, by and large, accept and expect divine interventions and miracles to occur as a natural expression of the articles of their faith. If we want to experience miracles in our lives, then we need to free up our model of reality in order to allow for their manifestation—not as isolated events, but as natural everyday expressions of our faith in the power of the realms of spirit, the morphic field of Zero Point energy that has been called, by some physicists, the Mind of God. If we do this consistently and coherently enough, we build the power station and string the cables of energy that allow for the conversion of unlimited energy to matter and back again—just as naturally, ultimately, as the act of drawing a breath.

Not to impress you, but rather to *impress upon you* the power and practicality of these ideas, I will tell you another story from my healing practice. Dave was a middle-aged Caucasian man. He smoked three packs of cigarettes a day and complained of heavy fatigue. This, of course, is not what brought him into my office. A friend of his who had experienced some amazing results with a back problem had referred him. Dave forgot to mention a few of his other complaints, since he thought it was not in the realm of possibility that they could be changed.

Remember what I have said. People will delete massive amounts of data if it doesn't pertain to the manner at hand. You generally get what you expect out of life. I have found that people's expectations can suck. Not to beat a dead horse, but what you ask consistently and congruently for, you will get. If you always focus on avoiding what you don't want, that has a way of attracting those things into your life as well. I am not speaking here about the power of positive thinking. You can say all sorts of positive affirmations to yourself, and visualize all good things coming to you. In my experience that is sometimes not enough to change things. Another deeper part of you may still be focused on what you don't want or think that you can't have. If you have a problem with self-*steam*, then opt for a different mode of transportation!

If everything in nature, including the quality of your thoughts and feelings, has a morphic resonance, then you need to choose extraordinary examples of what you want. Choose a role model until you roll up the old disgruntled self. Replace its essence with the values and qualities you would need in order to be the person who has what you truly want. *When you really know, and not just believe that you deserve it, you can have it.*

I can do the things that I do because I know that they will happen. I am not convinced; that can be a temporary and fleeting expression. I "know" in spite of what damaged or devalued parts of me might believe to the contrary. Yoda's words apply here: "You either do or do not, there is no try." If you merely try to do something, then you may fail. Do, with that part of you that knows you can, and it happens. And if it doesn't seem to happen right now, persist. One more thing: Let go.

My guides taught me to put pictures of people I admire—for what they can do and who they are—on my clinic walls where I can see them every day. Usually I am "told" who to include in my gallery of teachers and sources of inspiration. This is a very powerful form of an old technique of treasure mapping. When I want to either meet someone or have access to what they know and do, I am directed to put their picture on my wall. Currently, John of God is one of the countenances residing in a place of honor there.

Now it's time to get back to my story about Dave. He had a sacral vertebra out of place, and in this instance the best solution was a chiropractic adjustment. There was one little problem though; he couldn't lie down on the table. "Why not?" I asked. He then told me that for the last decade or so, ever since an ear infection, he had a problem with his balance. It had gotten so bad that he could not sleep on his back or right side without throwing up. He recently had taken to propping himself up on enough pillows that he slept in an almost sitting position. He had consulted countless specialists, all to no avail. In fact, the vertigo problem was so pronounced that he could not drive on winding side streets at all. Recently, he even had to be driven to his doctor appointments so he could prop himself up in a semi-reclined position in the back seat with his eyes closed. He had all but given up.

Now, "Whatcha gonna do? Who you gonna call? Paradigm busters!" Hear the music? Now, that is a great way to begin to shift your awareness to something useful. Music can be a great anchor to collapse those old patterns and thoughts. Did I feel particularly resourceful, or know that I could change that condition in that moment? Not on your life. So, whatcha gonna do, boy?

I looked up to my wall and fixed my gaze on John of God's picture. "He knows what to do," I thought. Assuming resonance with his morphic field, I reached up to Dave's nose and "saw" and felt myself as John of God. Without hesitation, in my mind's eye I inserted John's surgical clamp right up the man's nose and into his brain, just as I had seen in the video. Note, I didn't say that I imagined it; that would not be enough. Instantly, Dave slumped into unconsciousness, and I lowered him to my table *on his back*.

He came back to our world perhaps ten minutes later, finding himself staring up at the ceiling with absolutely no sign of his former condition. The vertigo was gone! He thanked me profusely, nearly in tears. I told him to thank John of God. He is the miracle man, not me. That old adage "Act as if until" can be really useful if you really embrace it and mean it. And no, the condition never came back. It was, after all, a miracle. Does that mean I can perform miraculous feats of healing on command? Absolutely not! A statement of Jesus comes to mind, who is for me the most powerful archetype for the miracle mind-set. "I CAN OF MINE OWN SELF DO NOTHING." Ditto. I am a perfectly imperfect vessel. God is the healer.

Experiencing New Realities

One way to really get the power of a new idea is to have an experience with an altered or non-consensus reality that takes you so far outside of your normal comfort zone that you experience a conversion of reality. When this happens you will, in some ways, never again view your existence with your now outgrown set of expectations. If something like this happens to you, then you have the choice of whether to tell others the details of your encounter with the unexpected and the extraordinary, or keep them to yourself, knowing full well that if you do share them some people might think you to be somewhat unbalanced of mind—in other words, "nuts." An example of this is the story of how Dr. Dunn was finally able to do this work.

It was the third year that Dr. Dunn had been training with me and it had not been an easy time for him. Sure, he learned a lot over the course of his time with me, but what he really wanted, what had originally excited him about studying with me, was "that thing that I did with my hands"—what became the system that I have called Matrix Energetics. With frustration mounting for both of us during that time, I had tried in every way possible to convey the essence of what he needed to know in order to duplicate my results and experiences. I have to admit that sometimes I wasn't the nicest of teachers either.

All good things must come to an end, and there were little hints in our relationship that Mark was approaching a breaking point where he could not, or would not, pursue the matter any further. The more he tried to duplicate my results with his small number of clients, the more vexed he would become and the harder he would try, all the while building a wall of frustration between himself and the desired outcome. I told him many times that he needed to turn that frustration into fascination, which would keep him in a more resourceful state. But he couldn't hear that at the time, and my saying so only seemed to frustrate him even more.

One Saturday morning the breaking point arrived. Mark wasted no time that day informing me of his feelings: "I have tried for three long years to do what you can do with your hands and I can't take it anymore. I give up! I'll give myself three more hours this morning, and if at the end of that time I still cannot do it, then that's it. I am finished with you. I quit. I can't take anymore. I am walking out that door and you will never see me again!" Though saddened inwardly at this tragic turn of events, I remained calm on the exterior, and holding up my wrist to look at my watch, said, "Okay then, I will check back with you in two and a half hours."

At the appointed time I made my way to Dr. Dunn's treatment room. As I approached the doorway, sounds of almost inhuman frustration were issuing forth from behind the closed door. The sounds were coming from my apprentice, and they did not bode well for our continuing relationship; in fact, this was the sound of a grim and ignominious defeat. With a tightly controlled sigh I opened the door, prepared to act out my final part in the play that had been running in my office for the last few years. Mark turned toward me, his face reddened with anger and self-reproach.

His hand was gesturing wildly toward his client, a woman who had come to him for relief from a painful shoulder injury. Voicing his years of pent up frustration, Mark said to me, "That! I just want to know what you would do with that!" and pointed to the woman's injured appendage. Always one to oblige, I waved my hand at the woman's shoulder and commanded "Move!" and it did, smoothly moving back into place with an audible crack.

With that sound came the breaking point for Mark. Unable to contain his frustration any longer, he held up his arms and practically shouted at me, "That's it! That's the final straw! You might as well just hit me!" Given the circumstances and knowing that something had to give right now or it was all over, I graciously acceded to what seemed a reasonable request from a desperate man, and I hit him square in the chest with a judiciously placed blow. With elegant precision, my student's feet left the ground and his body went sailing through the air to impact the far wall in that little room. The client watched all of this with eyes as round as saucers and growing apprehension. In the next few moments, Mark was to prove to me what he was really made of, because even though he was stunned by the impact of what had just transpired, he stood up and faced me with an enthusiastic posture and proclaimed with conviction, "Yeah! That's what I'm talking about. Again!"

Something significant was definitely happening here and a plan quickly took form in my mind as the air between us fairly crackled with anticipation and electricity. Facing my friend, I growled theatrically, "Enough is enough! I've had it with you and your density. I'm going to move your Assemblage point, sucker!"

If you have ever read Carlos Castaneda's tales of don Juan, you would understand the reference. In order to trigger a profound altered state in his student, don Juan hit Castaneda with his palm at a spot between his shoulder blades in order to move an energy pattern called the Assemblage point. Moving this construct would, theoretically, allow the recipient to move the focal point of his perceptions in order to enter into a shamanic trance in which other realities might be encountered and understood. Mark had also read these books, and I sensed that this was the moment we had both been waiting for; everything that had come before in his training had led us inexorably to this point at this exact moment. It was now or never. With no hesitation and all the chi and love I could muster, I once again delivered a powerful palm strike to his chest, giving my all to this moment in which I sensed a form of powerful magic at work.

Like in a scene from a Bruce Lee movie, I watched as Mark's feet left the ground in seeming slow motion and he flew, unfettered by gravity or earthly concern, his body impacting the opposite wall hard at the end of his short flight. He lay on the floor in a dazed trance, physically uninjured. I leaned forward so that my face was right in his and grabbed his hands, shoving them up into his line of sight. Then I growled at him, "See your hands glowing purple and be able to do this now!" With a dazed expression, Mark looked at his own palms and wonderingly replied, "My hands are glowing purple!" "Exactly," I snarled, as I turned on my heel and left the room. That was the turning point and he has been able to do what I do ever since!

So, as you read about Dr. Dunn's experience or the story in chapter 1 of what happened to me that opened my eyes to the possibility of a new version of reality, a new way of looking at the world, it's okay if you think that we're totally nuts. What I don't want you to do is to draw the conclusion that what happened to me in some way makes me special or "gifted." If you do that, you place artificial barriers between yourself and me and draw artificial distinctions, which can make it unnecessarily complicated or difficult for you to entertain the mind-set or state that makes the learning and practice of Matrix Energetics easy. My Superman experience simply opened my eyes so that I could see differently, feel differently, think in a new way, and experience my interactions of life with new awareness.

What I would like you to think about when reading my story is, "Gee, that story is a symbolic representation by his subconscious mind of archetypal forces, which represent the patterns of a mythology from his childhood. This is how his subconscious mind chose to represent information and experiences that were of an unfamiliar nature to him. That is interesting, and it says a lot about who he is; I wonder what I would experience if something similar were to happen to me?" If you do that while you are reading what I have to say, then you will make my story mean something to you, and hopefully that will be useful in your world. Then the story has a point, and perhaps can direct you toward an encounter with non-ordinary reality that will be uniquely significant to you. That way you will not limit yourself and your thinking; you will not turn me into somebody who can do this, while you can't.

What You See Is Not Always What You Get

Whenever I do demonstrations at events, what happens is so consistent that I absolutely can rely on the fact that certain effects will be readily demonstrated and easy to notice. It is good to have things that you can count on, don't you think? If you are on an icy road and it is snowing, you want to know that your snow tires will hold the road reasonably well. Equally, you want to know with a high degree of certainty that if you add two and two you will get four when using classical arithmetic.

When you see me in public demonstrations reproducing some of the effects that can happen with Matrix Energetics, please realize that what you see is only the tip of the iceberg. You may not be able to detect with your five senses all that is going on. I have had people email our website message board after witnessing one of my public events, saying, "He just laughed a lot and knocked a bunch of people to the ground, but I still have no idea what he does or what I can learn from him." Being able to knock someone to the ground or even to render them unconscious (a) means absolutely nothing in and of itself: It is merely an interesting phenomenon which, although consistent and reproducible, still means nothing at all; and (b) means everything. Assigning meaning to an experience is a very individual thing. We must decide for ourselves what a particular experience means, within the context of our own rules and perceptual filters for how we make sense of things that occur within the confines of our subjective reality.

It could mean everything if someone whom I demonstrate on goes into an altered state when I work with her, and perhaps even falls on the ground in a deep trance. She has the very grand opportunity, at the subconscious level, to assign a new meaning to that experience, since it probably falls outside the window of her normal daily expectations. In that moment, she could decide that this means that she can be healed of some medical condition, or that her relationship with her spouse will dramatically improve.

In one such instance, a seminar participant confronted me in the hallway before I went on to teach the very large class that was gathered there. She did not even ask me for anything in particular, which somehow works out for the best a lot of the time. When you don't assign a particular desire or need to the experience, anything can happen, since you have not in any way limited the outcome. She fell to the ground in a swoon, and then began laughing joyously, sounding like the peals of a great bell.

What the young lady related to me later was that she had always had a fear of crowds, as well as a strong case of claustrophobia, or fear of small and enclosed places. Later on during the first day of the seminar she found herself on the elevator, when normally she would have used the stairs. An older Japanese couple got on the elevator and seemed to be confused about what floor they were on, so the elevator continued to travel from floor to floor; she rode with them with nary a worry. When they got off at their floor she just kept going up and down in the elevator until she suddenly realized that she was enjoying the ride and felt no fear at all.

Later in the month, not content to accept that her phobia was truly gone, she did what would have formerly been unthinkable: On a family trip to Maui she went on an hour-long submarine tour of the ocean bottom at a depth of 190 feet. Even though space was very cramped on board the vessel and it was full to capacity with tourists, she had a splendid time with no hint of her former phobia at all. Now for the rest of the story, as radio icon commentator Paul Harvey says: The person in question is my daughter Justice, and I was with her on that submarine ride. I have to admit that I was less comfortable than she was.

Expectations Can Limit You

In order to deal with and meet the challenge of people's expectations, I tell them that an experience with Matrix Energetics can mean everything or can mean nothing: *no thing!* If you observe what I am doing as evidence that a particular thing has occurred, this in turn implies that by the power of your consciousness, your observation of one specific outcome, you may in turn limit the expression of all other possible desirable outcomes from the same experience. The act of choosing, as they say in quantum physics, collapses all the other probable occurrences into the one event or result that is consciously chosen. If I say that our interaction is about a "thing" then I have limited what "it" can be. In order to include all of the possibilities you have to consider what might normally be deemed impossible and make it part of the solution-set. If we interpret the ideas of quantum physics liberally and with a generous dose of imagination, we can begin to understand that for each possible outcome many other probability realities can occur—perhaps even some things that would be considered impossible within the context of our mutually assured construction of reality.

So within the framework of my interaction with the people at an event, many things may happen, even some that I do not consciously participate in. I have received calls and emails describing how, in a number of instances, someone in the audience had a healing event simply by sitting in the morphic field generated by the presentation. While this is obviously a very desirable occurrence, I can in no way promise that something of this nature will occur in any given set of circumstances; but nor will I be able to guarantee that it will not. Fortunately, those things are not entirely up to my conscious awareness or participation.

Expect the Unexpected

People will attach meanings to things. So whatever you see me do, you will see it through your own eyes and interpret it through your database of experiences. Each person might have a different experience, based on how you have set up the rules for deciding what things mean to you. Whatever meaning you make is ultimately only about you. Don't make it about faith healing, or knocking people to the floor. Also, don't think that if it doesn't happen, you are doing something wrong. That is just about how you interpret events within your worldview. You will see what you expect to see, and learn, in many cases, only within the context of what you already think you know.

Are You Ready to Wake Up in the Matrix?

Reach down and touch the surface of a table that is nearby. You probably think that when you touch the top of a table, its surface is hard and it is a solid, physical object. But really, the table is composed of a bunch of electrostatic charges that pop in and out of existence continually. If you learned to see the table from a quantum viewpoint or way of looking, perhaps if you could absolutely hold that desired state, you could put the fingers of your hand right through that tabletop. But don't try to do that if you see the table as a hard, fixed, structural object; you might break your hand!

Getting to a foothold in consciousness where experience in what others and I call non-ordinary reality is not only possible, but becomes second nature, requires constant practice in stretching the boundaries of your beliefs; then the flexibility of your new state practically demands that your experience of the world around you undergo a transformational shift. This is one of the things that I think the Matrix Energetics seminar does for those who attend. We provide a safe harbor for you to experiment and to map unusual, useful, and reproducible states of consciousness that can aid you in shifting the parameters of your awareness into a wavefront or quantum conscious state.

Once those state changes and new perceptions are accompanied by quantifiable experiences within the course of the seminar experiment, then you begin to experience confidence that this is something that is not weird, or "out there." It is merely another way of observing, which can and does produce physical changes in the people and things that you practice with. *Once the mind has stretched to encompass the reality of a new experience it can never shrink back entirely into the old way of seeing the world.* Like my example given earlier in this book, suddenly you look out into the previously empty harbor, but now you perceive the presence of "ships." What had been there, but was unperceived, suddenly appears obvious and just as real as anything else in your immediate environment. Welcome to day one of a new life's expression! This is what makes Matrix Energetics so much more than just a technique or system of healing.

PART 2

Getting "Two" the Point

B y DECIDING WHAT YOU ARE GOING TO EXPERIENCE and trusting that what one person has done anyone can do, you are "priming the pump" for success. Remember what you have read in this book: The act of deciding what and how to observe at the quantum level causes the object of your attention to behave or move in a fixed or predetermined manner. This is not merely a case of what has been called "mind over matter." No, this is an example of *mind as matter*; the two are one and the same, linked inextricably by the laser-like quality of your fixed attention on the object at hand.

Now I am going to teach you a preliminary exercise that will enable you to be successful at the Two-Point technique, which is the foundational tool for everything we do in Matrix Energetics.

Radionics is a form of distance healing in which numerical sequences represent subtle patterns of energy that can be used to analyze, as well as to correct, energetic imbalances in your personal health. Radionics has even been used to treat crops for insect manifestations and to increase crop yields. In the Radionics paradigm, you need to be able to analyze what to do in order to correct an energetic imbalance.

To do this, practitioners utilize something called a stick pad. The way this works is that you scan over a list of locations and problems while gently dragging your fingers across a stick plate. You are looking or feeling for your fingers to stick or stop moving when you locate the energy pattern that will correct the condition you are interested in. This is very easy to do with a little practice.

Go to a window or a tabletop and drag the fingertips of your right hand across its surface. The game that you are playing is to find some point on that surface where your fingers will stick and not move anymore. When you find that first point, hold it there; maintain the pull on the surface as your fingers continue to remain in contact with it.

Now drag the fingers of your other hand across the same surface area, looking for a point or area that makes those fingers stick as well. When you find it, tug your hand as it remains affixed to the surface in a vector or direction toward your first point, the one you previously located. Mentally link the two hands or points together. When you do this you create a connection that then allows you to perform a measurement; your photons are said to be "entangled," or linked. Practice this exercise on a number of different surfaces so that it is a very easy and natural thing for you to do. This prepares you for success in working on yourself or another person, place, or thing with Matrix Energetics.

With your focused observation or measurement of the two fixed points, you have entangled that information at the quantum level of light and information, creating a link between them. There are many areas that will work just as well as whatever two points you have chosen. There is no "right" point that you must be able to find and feel. Whatever you decide to use as your two points will work just fine, as long as you feel the connection or "pull" between them.

Getting to the Point

Just as you have already felt when working with the practice objects that you chose, you are now ready to duplicate the Two-Point process on yourself or someone else. First, you want to find an area of interest on yourself or the other person's body that feels stuck, rigid, or hard. Keeping one hand on your initial point, feel with your other hand until you locate a second point that makes the first point feel more rigid or stuck. I liken this feeling to the field of attraction that is created between two magnets with opposing poles when you hold them close together; there will be a pull or attraction between the two areas. This feeling or sensation is crucial to your success with this process. Use a fairly firm contact on your first point. It can be a painful area or just some location that your awareness is attracted to. If you move that area of the body while holding your first point, it may feel restricted in motion compared to what happens if you are not touching it. If you need help, watch the video clips on the internet, which have been filmed for this section of the book (www.matrixenergetics.com).

While firmly holding your first point, look for a second point somewhere on the body that, if you contact it, will make the first point feel slightly more rigid, hard, or immobile. Gently tug in a direction angled toward the first point, taking the tissues under your hand to tension. This action will make the two points feel connected, stuck together, or further restricted in motion. It is easier for a newcomer to pick either paired structures to compare, such as a point on the right shoulder and the identical point on the left shoulder. This allows you to note the differences in movement from side to side. Then, when you pick your first point on the problem or target area, you have a reference for how the normal side feels.

As you hold the two points, feel the connection between them. Feel and imagine that you are just working with photons or light. There is no body there, nothing solid except for your focus on the two points. The procedure that you learned with the table exercise can now be applied to working with yourself or someone or something else. You can imagine that you are linked and "entangled" with another person, or an area of yourself that you have chosen to focus on.

Some people find it easier to learn the Two-Point process by measuring movement. In my seminars I often choose an area on the top of someone's head, and then holding that first location, I move down the person's spine rocking them back and forth every few inches, demonstrating a very easily observed gross freedom of movement. When I find a second point that makes the first area feel more stuck, hard, or rigid, the spine will suddenly stop moving. This is very easy to demonstrate and readily visible to an audience. If you wish to see a demonstration of this principle in action, you can go to the website: www.matrixenergetics.com.

To remind you, two or more quantum systems can share the same quantum wave. When they do this, it can be said that they connect or become entangled. At the subatomic level you are made of high-energy photons; your body consists of light and information held in patterns or waves of interference. When you connect the two points, you have consciously observed them as being linked. You have created that link with your imagination. What you imagine at the level of the photon has tremendous power to change these patterns of light and information.

The act of focusing at this level, where everything is made of light energy, causes what you observe to behave differently. You collapse the particle-based arrangement of your world into intricate patterns or wavefronts of light. Feel and sense this happening.

Imagine what it would be like if you had no body and neither did the other person. Feel the space between you, the air around you, as only light waves of information that are merging. *Let go and allow the idea of "you" as separate from anything else to simply "go away" for a moment.* I know that sounds a bit cryptic, but it works really well. *This can happen the instant you stop thinking about it, if you give up trying to do anything, and you just are.*

That felt connection is real; you have created it by the focus of your attention on this process. Now imagine that the person's body and your body merge together as one thing, no longer separate. If you have ever thrown pebbles into a pond, think about what happens when the ripples intersect or connect. Feel what would happen in your imagination if you were to merge together as intersecting patterns of light. This activity is so natural that when you get accustomed to the feelings and sensations it produces, it will happen automatically with no need for conscious thought or conscious action. You don't think about the process of breathing, you just do it. This is as natural and easy as that, once you get used to it.

Notice What Is Different, Not What Is the Same

The way to train yourself to notice what has changed is to firmly hold on to your two points during the process, if possible. When you come back to solid-state particle awareness, feel the same two points again. Notice whether they feel softer or changed in some way after this process. Check to see if the area that you focused on has become more mobile, or perhaps less painful, if that was one of the criteria you used in your initial assessment of what to do.

One way to get better at this game is to feel the first point you originally chose, and while still holding it, move your other hand to another part of the body. You are looking for that same hard, fixed, stuck feeling. This will become your second point in another Two-Point procedure. Repeat the same steps again and check your results afterward. We call this step of observing what is different, calibration, or "tracking."

When you access the desired state, anything you do within the context of your intent will work. Of course, in any given situation some things will work better than others for you. When you feel the connection between the two points, there is really nothing to do! This is why we have somewhat playfully called this second step "The Art of Not Doing." The Art of Not Doing is a term that I have borrowed from the writings of Carlos Castaneda.

What I teach is that when you really enter into the state that is Matrix Energetics, you simply "are" and there is nothing to "do." Some of my best clinical outcomes have occurred when I got out of the way, engaging "No Mind" in the interplay with "No Matter," so that all things were open as a possible outcome. When done in this way, though hard to grasp with left-brain monkey logic, "Nothing" really does work better, as the drug ads often claim.

Methods for Collapsing the Wave

Now, on the subject of consciousness collapsing the wave, I have to be honest with you in saying that there really is nothing to collapse. We're not really "doing" anything. We hold a focused intent in our minds and a larger force or power manifests through that intent. Engaging the conscious mind with a process of visualization is a great way to get it out of the way, so the real work of "doing nothing" can take over.

The eminent mathematician John von Neumann stated, "Consciousness collapses the wave," an expression that we use to explain how something that is apparently a solid physical object can be transformed into wavefront patterns, and then reconfigured as a new physical outcome moments later. When I say consciousness collapses the wave, this is a metaphor for what happens when we perform this work. It in no way implies that we know what really happens; it is just my way of trying to explain the inexplicable.

When you practice the art of Two-Point, it represents a new paradigm for things that you can do or access with your sensory modality of touch. If you endeavor to do this on a daily basis, you begin to have glimpses of the hidden reality and its complexities behind the shroud of daily events. Things no longer happen to you. Instead, you begin to take responsibility for your creative use of universal energy.

If you do this, you begin to understand what Dr. William Tiller was talking about when he said, "Since every application of our intention is an act of creation, it ultimately teaches us how to create properly, efficiently, and effectively. This in turn ultimately manifests in some type or types of events in our sensory world." Keeping in mind that Dr. Tiller is not some wild-eyed "New Age" metaphysician, but one of our elder statesmen of physics, you begin to grasp the scope and the depth of the possibilities embedded within what he is saying.

Yes, I know he's saying, "You create your own reality." Has it ever been said so elegantly and precisely? When I focus my imagination on this process for the purpose of observing and engineering a physical change, I am, through an act of will, creating a new outcome. This is how I have set up the "rules" for my reality. With repeated practice the whole process becomes so streamlined that it requires little to no conscious thought or effort. It just naturally happens.

In effect, I am imposing or constraining an act of conscious creation to conform to the parameters of the template that I have created. If I were to limit this outcome by merely focusing on the "treatment" of some physical condition, then that is all that would change as a result. By releasing this created template to perform its perfect work, I leave the door ajar for the principle of Grace to act in a manner that may well be beyond my capacity to imagine.

It is helpful to think that when you are doing the Two-Point procedure with someone else, you are in a very real way entangled with some aspect of yourself. Your experience of the other person is not the same as their experience of themselves, or even their experience of you. It is a uniquely blended state, and when you engage in the production of such an outcome there is a unique opportunity for the transformation of consciousness to occur. Through this process, not only do the things that you choose to focus on change, but you change and transform as well. By doing nothing, and not trying to fix anything during this process, you are entering into transformation.

Although "seeing is believing" for some of us, results speak for themselves and need no external witness in order to verify them. You do need some way, though, to notice a change that helps you to track the external part of an event, which of course has much greater ramifications at deeper levels than anything you can consciously observe or notice. The Two-Point process allows you to do this. If you have found two points, and you notice changes in how they feel after you have merged with the information and come back to solid-state, particle awareness, congratulations on your entry into a more magical and awe-inspiring world!

In my seminars, or at another of my events, you might see incredible-looking demonstrations where people's physical structures or their symptoms change rapidly. It is a natural occurrence for more than one person to wind up in an altered state on the floor over the course of the evening. Although big demonstrations are fun and help you to see and to believe in the power of the work, they are not necessary. Sometimes, during the best work that I have done, nothing outwardly appeared to happen. The changes can be subtle in the physical realm, and yet a person's whole experience of reality can shift as a result. If you want to see me in action, check out the clip of me demonstrating this process on the Matrix Energetics website (www.matrixenergetics.com).

Please do not try to duplicate what you see me do on the website without first attending our Level One seminar. The phenomenon in which you see people being assisted to the floor is largely for demonstration purposes, although this also happens with some regularity in my private practice as well.

The Art of Feeling Stuff

When you practice the art of the Two-Point, it represents a new paradigm for things that you can do or access with your sensory modality of touch. If you endeavor to do this on a daily basis, you will begin to glimpse the hidden reality and its complexities behind the shroud of daily events. Things no longer happen *to* you. Instead, you begin to take responsibility for your creative use of universal energy, your life, and what you experience as direct feedback concerning what you have set in motion in the past.

I would like to emphasize that this *is really not a physical process*, and it also has nothing to do with the conventions associated with the concept many energy or light workers use of "running energy." This process is virtually instantaneous most of the time, although the ramifications or effects of the Two-Point and the other procedures that I teach can definitely "play out" over time. If you observe this process as taking time, or you think that you are running energy, then your experience with Matrix Energetics will be limited to what you expect to see or experience.

Finding two points serves two practical purposes. First, it gives you something to measure, in order to be able to notice what is different when something changes. Through the act of observing or measuring what changes, you are learning to calibrate and replicate what a successful outcome looks and feels like.

Second, this exercise in imagination serves to engage you with the other person, but not as a physical body. You are interacting within complex interlocking patterns or holographic representations of energy organized and driven by consciousness. By focusing on the qualities of the two interconnected points, your imagination enters into this process and serves as a focus for your intent. With our imaginations playfully engaged, we then can learn to move into a state of nothing, an empty set free of limitations that allows for greater and more powerful outcomes. *When we can embrace the Nothing, we gain access to the All.*

Two-Point Review

1. Locate a point on your body or a partner's, which, when you touch it, feels stuck, hard, or rigid.

2. Find a second point which, when held in relation to the first point that you are still touching, makes the relationship

between points one and two feel even more taut, or perhaps even as if there is a magnetic attraction between the two areas.

3. Forming a somewhat arbitrary link between these two points allows for a measurement to be made. Remember that according to quantum theory you cannot observe something without becoming entangled or interacting with it. The very act of observing the connection between these points with your feeling/imagination makes it so. This entangles the data, and in effect, collapses the wave of matter/consciousness that you have chosen to observe and to interact with.

4. Notice what is different now. The area between your two points probably feels softer and less rigid. You may notice changes in respiration; you or your practice partner may feel hot or flushed. It is not uncommon for the body to begin to sway or move to the beat of some unconscious primal rhythmic force. Stand behind your partner, because if you really have entered the state that I am describing he or she may even momentarily lose consciousness. It is good to be prepared for anything, including spontaneous laughter, crying, or some other form of emotional/physical release.

KEY POINTS TO REMEMBER

1. It takes at least two points to measure anything.

2. In order to learn something new, you begin by noticing what is different.

3. Noticing what is different helps you suspend critical judgment and allows space for a new pathway of least action to be created. (In other words, you are creating a new activity that, with practice, becomes a new skill.)

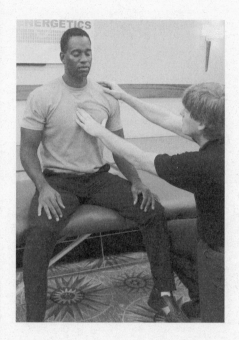

1A: Two-Point Example

This shows a standard issue Two-Point. My first point is the top of the left shoulder and my second point is the middle of his sternum. Feel the energy—in each of these photos I am really doing something.

1B: Two-Point Example

My right hand has a broad contact on his head. The second point in this example is an acupuncture point called HO-KU or LI4. This combo could be used for a symptomatic treatment of a headache. This one is easy to do on yourself.

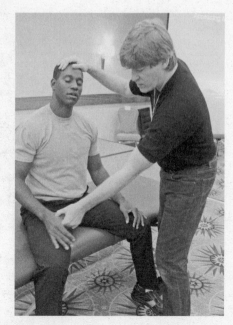

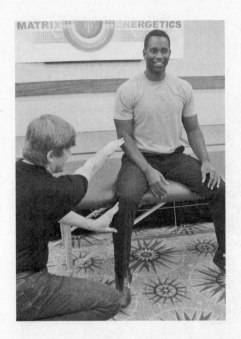

1C: Two-Point Example

Here I demonstrate something I might do with a knee problem. The first point is actually on the knee and my second point is on the elbow. This demonstrates the conceptual flexibility of the Two-Point process. Remember to feel the connection between your two points. Feel the energy coming out of his chest area; it is very expansive and happy.

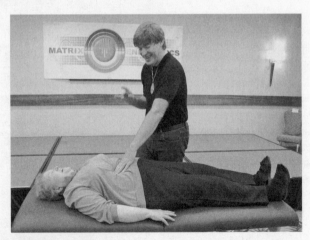

1D: Two-Point Example

The liver is on the right side of the body and can be accessed at the bottom of the rib cage. My second point is in the air, what you could call her aura. The happy smiles on our faces are due to the intense, wonderful, and connective energy we have established with the Two-Point.

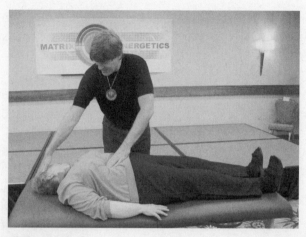

1E: Two-Point Example

I am still holding the first point, while my second point has moved to her head. In Chinese acupuncture, liver chi problems can be associated with depression and certain forms of migraine headaches. Really, I just felt like touching her head for my next point and trusted that!

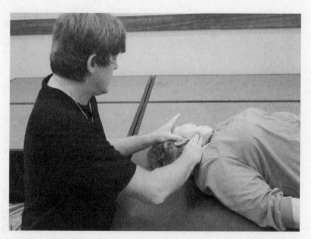

1F: Two-Point Example

This could be an example of working on TMJ. My first point is on the jaw joint and my second is a tooth in this case. Don't make the mistake of thinking I am showing you the way to do something; these are just examples, and whatever you see or make up will work just fine.

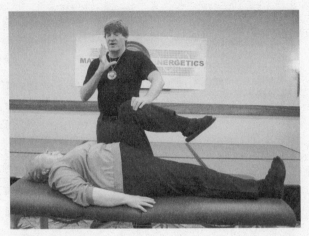

1G: Two-Point Example

I am playing with a knee, while accessing the quantum energy field. Feel the connection in and around yourself when you do something like this. Remember, I am not running energy here; the connection is immediate and instantaneous. This is a great way for you to work on yourself!

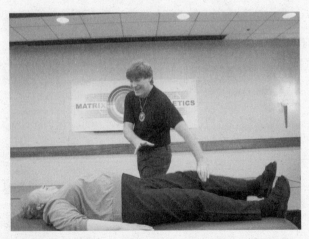

1H: Two-Point Example

Same first contact. If you know about chakras, this might be an example where my second point is the field of the second chakra, which is often associated with emotions. Happy times—the energy we are creating between us feels great!

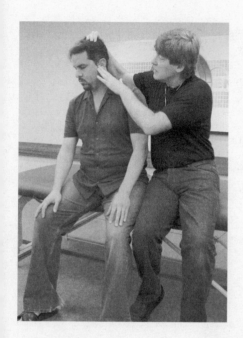

1I: Two-Point Example
He is in bliss! Another example of me touching the head or jaw. Keep in mind that even though I am touching two points on his head, we might be focusing on the intent of shifting his finances or improving his love relationships.

2A: Two-Point Sequence
I am holding her head just to control the response. You can see very big physical responses with the Two-Point. She might have tension between her shoulders, or perhaps an upset stomach. Whatever two points you choose to notice will work just fine. You do not have to touch the "problem" area in order for it to change. Your mind can link up with that.

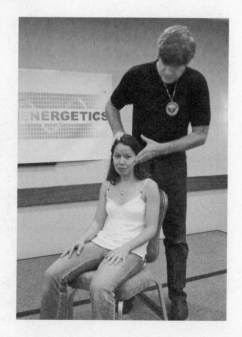

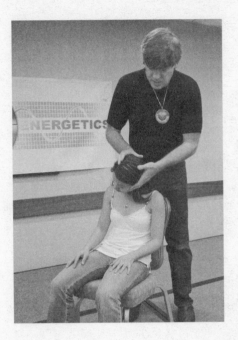

2B: Two-Point Sequence
Feel the quantum wobble in this picture. Do not attempt to drive while looking at this picture. When you collapse the wave of the pattern that you desire to change, other things can collapse as well.

3A: Two-Point Sequence
This is an example of head-to-heart integration. Very peaceful. Physical contact is not necessary but allows the practitioner to track or physically feel the changes in real time. I could be working on an incident from her childhood with the Time Travel Technique or harmonizing her for a food allergy. The chosen contacts are not important—the intent is!

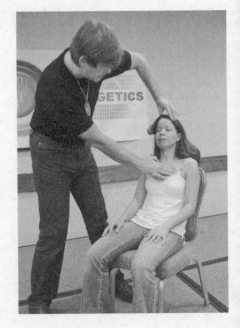

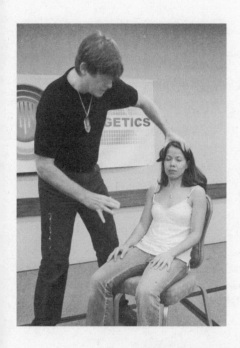

3B: Two-Point Sequence

Here we track changes in her energy field. We are connected via the concept of quantum entanglement, and we are both changing as a result of our interaction. You can feel the energy of the space between us. Look at this picture and pay attention to what *you* notice.

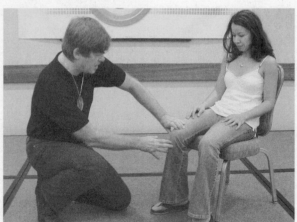

4A: Two-Point Sequence

My first two points here are working with her knee. However, consider the idea that we might be focusing on an issue such as menstrual cramps and that the knee is just the physical entry point we have chosen to utilize.

4B: Two-Point Sequence

The knee is moving physically beneath my hand while my second hand works in her energy fields. Always feel the connection or link between the two areas that you have chosen. It feels a little like the opposite poles of a magnet attracting the two points together.

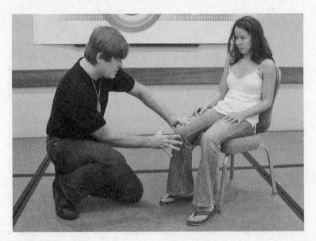

4C: Two-Point Sequence

I am re-checking what has changed from our Two-Point procedures. The act of measuring the change conceptually solidifies your results. Measuring the difference after what you have done teaches you how to be more efficient and powerful and streamlines the entire process.

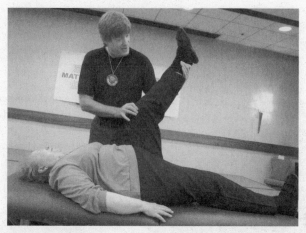

5A: Two-Point Sequence
This could be an example of swelling in an ankle. Even though she is older, we might "Time Travel" back to a sprain she had when she was four years old as our initial "chess move" in this sequence. When I contact the second point on the knee, it makes the ankle point feel harder, tense, or rigid, signifying that we have successfully connected our two points.

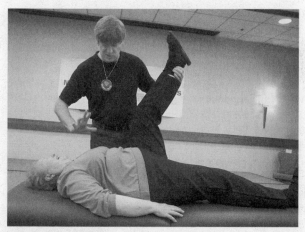

5B: Two-Point Sequence
While I am still holding my first point at the ankle, the energy has now shifted to around the chest or heart area. We are both feeling the energetic expansion resulting from the Two-Point process.

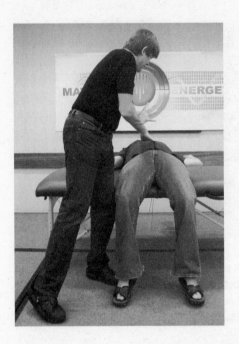

6A: Two-Point Sequence

This picture shows how dynamic the effects of the Two-Point can be. I am holding one hand as my first point on his chest and feeling the response in that point to what I am tracking with my second contact, which is in his energy field over the heart. When mathematician von Neumann stated, "Consciousness collapses the wave," he wasn't kidding!

7A: Two-Point Sequence

This is a huge state of energy between us. If you could stand in the space between our two bodies I am sure you could feel it. Why don't you mentally put yourself there now and notice whatever you may feel? The molecules of the air around us seem alive with power and purpose!

7B: Two-Point Sequence
This photo is taken just moments later. The results of this interaction could potentially be life-changing for both of us!

8A: Two-Point Sequence
Animals are not burdened by opinions or skepticism. They just *are*. Matrix Energetics works great with them or even with so-called inanimate objects such as your car.

8B: Two-Point Sequence
Here is a clearly demonstrated Two-Point.

8C: Two-Point Sequence
Like Nicholson's Joker in the first *Batman* movie, "I get a grin again!" This dog is riding the wave to a happy place!

8D: Two-Point Sequence
WOW!

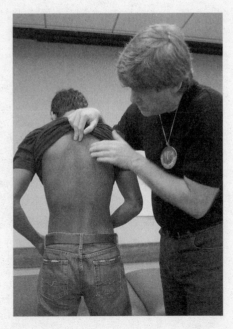

9A: Two-Point Sequence
Locating my first point on his back. These next two pictures demonstrate how easy it is to correct scoliosis or curvatures of the spine. Anyone can do this, as well as everything else I teach. No knowledge of anatomy or healing techniques is required.

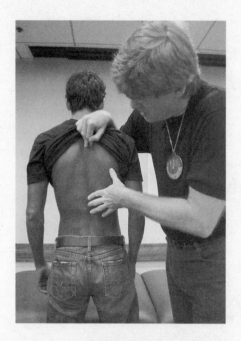

9B: Two-Point Sequence
The second point chosen will make the first point feel harder, fixed, or rigid beneath your point contacts. Remember to feel the connection between the two points as well as between yourself and the person, place, or thing. He had a curvature, which corrected the moment I touched him with the two points.

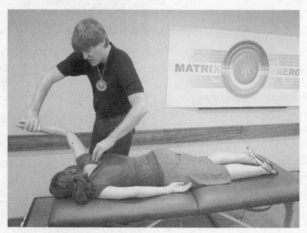

10A: Two-Point Sequence
I am Two-Pointing a painful shoulder. My second point is on the wrist of the hand I am holding.

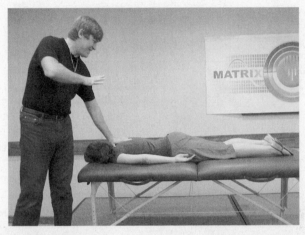

10B: Two-Point Sequence
After my initial Two-Point, my second point shifts into the energy field above her body. I am still holding my first point on her body, anchoring and allowing me to feel the changes that occur.

11A: Two-Point Sequence
Here is a straightforward Two-Point for foot or ankle pain. Would you like "pointers" for dealing with plantar fascitis?

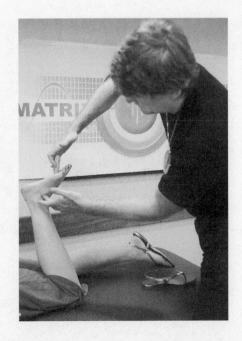

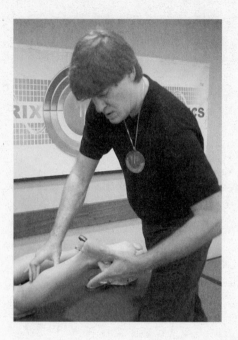

11B: Two-Point Sequence
Here is the follow-up sequence. Still holding the ankle point, my second contact has moved to a location in the calf muscle. Remember, your second point could have been anywhere on her body or even the surface of the massage table. The important thing is to feel the connection.

12A: Two-Point Sequence
Children love Matrix Energetics. This girl was a seminar attendee at a recent event. She taught the grown-ups a thing or two about the power of active imagination.

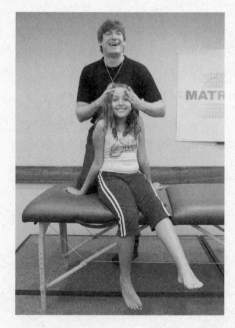

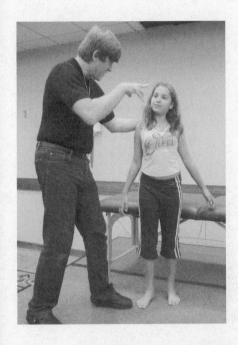

13A: Two-Point Sequence
Working in the consciousness grid.

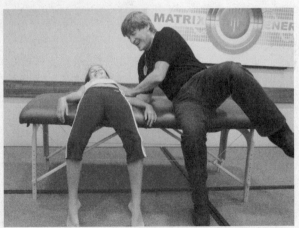

13B: Two-Point Sequence
This wave took us both out! Surf's up, Big Kahuna!

14A: Tigger-Point Therapy

My daughter Justice is demonstrating a Two-Point on herself by using Tigger as a surrogate. She is working on her sacrum, and her second point is on her head. This could be just as easily done on someone at a distance, using a surrogate to represent the person. Your focused intent is what makes the connection.

14B: Two-Point Yourself

Justice is demonstrating working on an emotional issue here. She is holding her first point on her chest. Her second point is a felt connection with her first point in her energy field.

14C: Two-Point Yourself
In another method for doing work with yourself, Justice is imagining a three-dimensional, life-size holographic representation of herself and holding her two points on this template.

14D: Two-Point Yourself
This is an easy way to work on a headache or head injury.

Let It Just Happen

In Chinese philosophy the concept behind Matrix Energetics might be called Wei Wu Wei, roughly translated as action/non-action. The mind and its myriad thoughts stand still and the pool of water can then be clear. This state is very similar to the goal of most forms of meditation. When you are able to still your thoughts, you come into resonance with the great sea of universal energy, or Zero Point Field. Of course, upon reading this please do not make the mistake that you must meditate to be able to "do" Matrix Energetics, for this is simply not so. If this were a requirement I am sure this energy/spirit would never have chosen me. My mind is rarely still; indeed, I have been called "the poster child for Ritalin"!

Don't obsess on whether or not you are doing it right. Stop trying so hard to understand how it is done and just let it happen. Don't say to yourself, "Let me draw a line between those two points; uh-oh, my line is crooked, I had better start again. Let me measure that line—is that in centimeters or inches; I wonder if it matters?" You can get so caught up with your thoughts, you can't think anymore—and *that* is usually when the change happens.

The moment that you stop actively thinking, you can become one with the object of your thought. You are entangled from a quantum perspective and that is when the shift occurs. When this event takes place, note it unconsciously. Allow yourself to be surprised, delighted, and empowered all at the same time. Congratulations! You have just expanded the mind's window and taken a giant step into a larger world of possibility.

The point is that the points do not really mean a thing outside the meaning you assign them. Why not just make it up to mean that here is one reality, and it is intersecting and merging with this other reality to create something new and wonderful? And be respectful of your own unique process.

One example I like to use taken from my own clinical practice amply illustrates this point. One day a gentleman came to see me for elbow tendonitis and plantar fascitis. He had elbow pain and pain on the bottoms of his feet. I thought to myself, "All right, I get it, you're a guy. You want me to treat your symptoms. Okay, I'll play along." So I spent about two minutes on his elbow, and perhaps a total of five minutes working with his feet. At the end of that time he told me that they didn't hurt anymore. I looked at the clock and realized that we still had almost thirty minutes left.

I held up my right hand in his energy field, about a foot away at chest level, and focused my awareness on nothing in particular. Moments later he slumped over, unconscious, lying across my massage table. His whole body began to shake violently as if he were having a seizure or something. However, if this was a seizure it was unlike the clinical presentation of any I had ever witnessed. He had a beatific expression on his face. The rest of his first encounter with me consisted of me holding my hand out in his energy field, while he continued to gently smile and shake. Unconcerned, I watched this, feeling a tremendous sense of love and well-being welling up in my heart.

He came back to see me a few weeks later and reported happily that the symptoms he had originally come in for were mostly gone. He did report some slight right elbow pain and he told me that I could work on it if I liked, but he had something else that he really wanted to talk with me about. With a puzzled frown on his face and in a gentle voice, he began to tell me about what had happened since his first visit.

He told me that he felt really great after leaving the office and had had hardly any pain since. But the morning after, he woke up and felt really sad, sadness he had rarely felt before, and this feeling lasted all day. On the morning of the second day, he felt energized and full of joy, as if some cosmic battery with an inexhaustible supply had been switched on in his heart. He paused after telling me this and then his face broke into a huge grin as he continued, "And on the third day I felt 'enlightened,' and I don't even know what that is!"

I inquired of him what he wanted me to focus on. He looked down at his formerly injured elbow, admitting that it still hurt "just a little," but then he said, "Could I have more of that incredible energy again?" Beaming, I held up my right hand, palm toward his heart, and he fell across my table again, and began having another one of those kundalini/seizure-like episodes. A deep smile that seemed to radiate from within played across his face. This truly is about Transformation. I was overjoyed once again that my life is so blessed that I get to witness and be part of events like these.

What does it all mean? I don't know. If I got into my Firebird and had to know how the engine actually functioned mechanically in order to be able to drive, I probably would not be going anywhere anytime soon. This, of course, is not to say that I cannot operate a motor vehicle. Those are two different things entirely.

Reinventing Yourself

The following stories about Matrix Energetics and using the Two-Point technique have come from students all over the world, via email and the internet. I am sharing them with you to provide examples of the multitude of ways in which Matrix Energetics is useful and can be usefully applied.

From the time I was nine years old I had a blockage of energy in my solar plexus. It was, or felt like, a very concentrated collection of negative energy. Every time I did any soul searching or meditation, it seemed to become worse. The first time I attended one of your demo nights you called me up on stage. When I went back to my seat it became much, much more pinpointed and powerful. I couldn't leave with it like that, so after you had finished talking I asked you to help. By the end of the evening it felt better than it had for years. It wasn't completely gone, though. I did my best to focus on noticing what was different. Three days later, it dawned on me that I had been approaching it from the wrong perspective for years. I had seen it as a blocked pipeline, so I tried to push the energy out. Without any conscious effort I thought, "What would it be like if it just flipped out of this reality?" Instantaneously, it was completely gone. It hasn't returned.

I hadn't even been to a seminar at this point, but I didn't need any more convincing after that. I realize only the last bit was my doing, but I hope this helps!

—*Samantha*

A couple of weeks ago at work the phone calls were coming too fast and furious. My colleagues and I were being overwhelmed. I Two-Pointed the situation and the phone calls completely stopped. We had time to catch up with the patient referrals we already had. There was even time to get the fliers ready for our annual Rose Show. Next, I made personalized fax cover sheets for our new team member. I even had time to clean up files, and so on. I guess it got too quiet. The Executive Director walked into our corral as we were all chatting. She wondered why the phones weren't ringing. A few minutes later the Hospice Director came into our area. She also asked, "Why is it so quiet?"

Then she turned and looked at me and said "Sara, I want these phones ringing right now." I sighed, Two-Pointed again, and said the phones would start up again within two minutes. My colleagues all sighed too, because they know by now whenever I Two-Point, things happen. The break was nice—the phones rang like crazy for the rest of the day.

And Today's Two-Point:

Three of us were driving to our Matrix Energetics study group in Berkeley today. We needed to get across the Bay Bridge and the traffic kept getting worse. We were creeping along as we approached the bridge. Bill called 511 to check on the traffic. It said that there was an overturned tractor-trailer blocking the left lane approaching Treasure Island and traffic was backed up past 7th Street. I looked up and saw the sign for 7th Street! We had planned to get to Berkeley in time to get coffee before the study group.

I said we should just Two-Point the situation. We all did our thing... suddenly all the cars sped up, there was no congestion, and we never saw the overturned tractor-trailer. I asked each person what he or she had done. I had done a simple Two-Point to the other side of the bridge. Samantha had Two-Pointed and saw a wormhole for us to drive through. Bill Two-Pointed with the intent of having time for a cappuccino before the study group. We had our coffees and were still early.

—*Sara*

I used the Two-Point the other day when I was in my forest talking to the rhodies that are blooming in there. The mosquitoes were voracious! I said to them, "Now look here, I don't want to have to kill you." It didn't work. I sent a message to the Mosquito King: "Get your people away from me." That didn't work either. Finally, I Two-Pointed a space of six inches around me, and that worked. I wasn't bitten again in the remaining ten minutes I was in the forest.

Willie was trying to figure out how to Matrix the lawn. Nothing worked. It still needed cutting. Then he Two-Pointed between himself and our helper, and suddenly all of the weed whacking was done (by the helper). Now, this may seem to be a silly story and it is sort of a joke. But for me, it points out how Matrix Energetics allows a person to notice that their options can expand. In pre-Matrix syndrome, Willie wouldn't have thought of the technique called "Ask."

Last but not least: After my first seminar, I knew I had to go to more seminars, even if I had to walk to get there. I Two-Pointed between myself and the seminar, seeing a golden cord binding me to the teaching. So seamlessly that one could scoff that it had nothing to do with my Two-Point (and one did), money suddenly started showing up, allowing me to attend four more times. We have barely scratched the surface of what Matrix Energetics can do. Deepest love and gratitude.

—*Nancy*

My husband David and I met you in San Diego, and I've flown a client up to San Rafael to see you . . . wonderful healings have happened as a result. One story I can share is about our happy dog JakJak, who right after the SD seminar very suddenly began having dark red yellowish blood in his urine. We were alarmed, and took him to our very competent vet who thought it might be a kidney, prostate, or liver-related issue. She did some tests, which came back positive for a serious liver problem; this was a shock, because he's only three years old, and we were reminded of a former dog we'd lost several years ago that died of a congenital kidney disease. While JakJak was in the hospital, David and I decided to do Matrix Energetics remote healing on Jak from home, since like prayer (just another form of energy!) it sometimes works better in groups. I've been raised doing remote healing work since childhood, and adding the Matrix Energetics cross-pollinated frequencies and modules was an efficient way to play with the idea of inviting back the former vibe of a healthy, happy, vibrant Jak.

I could hardly wait until the next morning to check in with the vet. When I called her she sounded a little hesitant, and insisted on keeping Jak another day, saying that a weird thing had happened. I asked her what was up. She said that although the tests had come back positive for lots of bilirubin in the dark red bloody urine, when they took Jak outside for a pee that morning, his urine looked absolutely normal and clear—no traces of blood at all. She could not understand this, and wanted to run another test to make sure he was okay... or not. Well, long story short, he was fine. No problem, just like that. When I went to pick him up, she asked me what I was using with Jak, since she knows the work my husband and I do, and asked me to continue doing whatever it is, and good luck! Good Luck, indeed! Thanks to all of you who continue to share your Light and Love.

—*Robin*

When I wake up in the morning and sometimes feel some ache and pain in my back, a quick Two-Point will usually eliminate the problems. Also, Two-Pointing my head and neck in the morning to realign myself with gravity is helpful. I also find it works when I feel I'm getting stressed. Pain after excessive work-out can be fixed by Two-Pointing. I have also had great success in increasing my flexibility, which is improving my tai chi and yoga practice. For this purpose, Two-Pointing with Time Travel works best for me while targeting the problem area. Regards.

—*Tom*

When I run into tables, slam my finger in the drawer, or drop things on my foot, I immediately Two-Point, go back in time prior to the incident, and the bruise/pain vanishes.

—*Jill*

A week before this month's seminar in Los Angeles, I found my dog throwing some type of a fit in the kitchen. First, I naturally panicked—my stomach sank into the floor while he was convulsing, not breathing, and looking terrible. At that moment, I truly thought that he was going to die, but somewhere during all of the chaos I stuck my hand in his mouth (making sure he didn't swallow his tongue), and the infamous "Two-Point" popped into my head. Like a prayer to God, I put my hands (after removing one from his mouth) on his head and back, and pictured him running around like he normally did. Within two or three minutes he started to lightly pant, still wobbly and falling over, though. In less than ten minutes he went back to his normal behavior. The profound thing about this was that I had no way of driving him to the vet in that condition. So, at that point, I knew my mediator was the "Two-Point," which ended up being my shift in awareness: from chaos to a new reality.

—*Tigeress*

My first experience using a Two-Point for myself was on the return trip from my first seminar in San Diego. I was driving home in the rain and noticed that my windshield wipers were not working very well (especially the one on the driver's side). I knew that I could not drive the rest of the way home that way and decided to try using a Two-Point. First I began with the weather. I Two-Pointed no rain until I could get my wiper replaced. Then I Two-Pointed an auto supply store on the right side of the freeway, with easy on/off access and my blades in stock. I also added that if I could not find one before, there would be one at the off-ramp I had chosen as a gasoline stop. Well, within five minutes, the rain had stopped. As I drove down the freeway I imagined what might be going on in the universe—were elves building an auto supply store somewhere down the road? Could the people who were driving by see what was going on? Was it just not there one minute and suddenly there the next? What was there before, an open space? Another business? What must that do to the people who work there? What a strange day they must be having. I hope they know something about auto parts.

It took about forty-five minutes, and there on the right side of the road was a huge towering sign for an auto supply store. It was conveniently located near an easy on/off-ramp and they had my blades in stock. Not only that, but the sky opened a bit and I changed my blades in full sunshine. I deliberately looked at the clock to see what would happen, and literally within four minutes after I pulled out of the parking lot, it began to rain. The best part is that later on, when I got off the highway for gas, there was an auto supply store right next to the gas station too! Those elves must have been very busy. Now that I have been to two more seminars, I have learned that maybe it would have been easier to just Two-Point the blade, but I was still so happy with the results. Blessings.

—*Sandy*

After my first seminar in March, I Two-Pointed her [my daughter's] tummy and the future her, holding a tiny baby in her arms. Of course, she is now pregnant, quite soon after I did this Two-Point. Oh, I also used an archetype of Mother Goose laying an egg on her tummy. Not your typical Chinese Medicine!

—*Gina*

I am a massage therapist and I was working on my client for almost three years. She had a stroke, and after the stroke she started to limp. My friend does Matrix Energetics work so I sent my client, who was limping, to her. Twenty minutes later, my client came out of the room and guess what? She was not limping at all. I asked my client what she [the Matrix friend] had said. She told me, "She was counting my years, I fell back on the floor, I got up, and the pain in one knee is gone and I am not limping."

When I decided to go to San Francisco to learn Matrix, the first day I thought, okay, those teachers are aliens. On the second day I thought, they are really crazy! On the third day I said, okay, now I am crazy! On the fourth day I said how wonderful it is to be crazy and see that it WORKS! Now I am opening my car's door when I can't turn the key by doing Two-Pointing and taking my car back in time to when it was made. How crazy is that?!

—*Karina*

7

Archetypes

ANOTHER WAY TO WORK WITH MATRIX ENERGETICS is to use the idea of working with symbols or archetypes. The language of the right brain is based in symbols and pictures. Now, there are a number of ways to incorporate what I call archetype technique into your therapeutic "wave." One way is to utilize primal geometric shapes, such as circles, spheres, triangles, rectangles, and squares. If you are really feeling adventurous, you can opt for more complexity by working with tetrahedrons, octahedrons, or in fact, any shape.

However, if you did not particularly excel at geometry in school, there is another, more natural way to do the same thing. In this approach, you just work with the first image that comes to mind. While constructing your wave and focusing your intent, mythological gods, cartoon figures such as Bugs Bunny, Superman, or any shape or image can spring to mind unbidden. I like to tie this to the idea that has been referred to as "skimming," where the object of the game is to just notice whatever catches your attention and then work with that.

In Joe McMoneagle's book, *Remote Viewing Secrets*, he advocates that when learning to access the skill of remote viewing you can greatly facilitate the process by paying attention to how things are presented to your conscious mind. Archetypal shapes and patterns, as well as more complex visual representations, may be utilized. Whatever you see or imagine is just perfect. Use whatever readily presents itself to your mind's eye. By paying attention to and honoring the patterns of thought that are offered to you in symbolic form, you begin to build a bridge between right- and left-brain functioning. These spontaneous images and patterns can be used to harmonize the two halves of the brain. Practice with this method can begin to unite the two hemispheres, creating and sustaining greater coherence and harmony: a goal of most meditative techniques.

When you open your awareness to these spontaneous and often playful images, you are gaining access to a much greater database than is normally presented to you by your conscious mind. The conscious mind is like a gatekeeper whose job is to filter and delete any information that doesn't fit the paradigm of what could be called a "need to know basis." If the information appears irrelevant or not in step with consensus reality expectations, then it is usually relegated to the "back room" of your subconscious. It can process something along the magnitude of eleven million bits of data per second, compared with the left brain's paltry sum of seven bits per second (plus or minus two bits). *So pay attention to your flashes of intuition and your hunches, for they are likely to be based on far more information than that of your normal conscious state.*

I can almost hear some of you thinking, "Well, that's great for him, but I could never do that; I can't visualize and I have never been psychic at all!" That is just what the wife of a famous chiropractor told me. I stopped her before she could get too worked up and I asked her a simple question. "Close your eyes and tell me, can you imagine what the inside of your house looks like?" "Of course," she replied. I then asked her, as her eyes remained closed, if she could picture the route that she and her husband had driven in order to come to the seminar, and again she nodded in the affirmative.

At this point I leaned over and whispered in her ear, "You certainly have proven to me that you have a great imagination; just think about all of the things that you used to imagine you could not do, only to find out that when you tried them they were quite easy. I see no difference here." She opened her eyes and focused on me with a somewhat dazed smile. "You are right, I just haven't given myself permission to play with a new idea! I am going to just relax and play and see what happens." With that announcement she then went off to lunch.

When the seminar reconvened after lunch she was waving her hands at me, bouncing up and down excitedly, and obviously experiencing great delight. I called her to come up on the stage and tell everyone present what was so exciting. She told the group about our earlier conversation and then proceeded to say that she had a life-transforming event occur while she was at lunch. She had been eating a large green salad, what her husband often playfully referred to as "rabbit food," when suddenly just as she was raising her fork to her mouth to take a bite she felt an odd quivering sensation on the side of her face. Curious, she wondered what it could be, when suddenly she realized that she had transformed her awareness in such a way that she was experiencing what it was like to be a rabbit. The quivering on the side of her face was her whiskers!

Now, as silly as all this sounds, she was absolutely thrilled. She knew that this experience was a gentle and amusing prompting from her subconscious mind. She *did* have a very powerful imagination. Suddenly, it was all right to experience something that just didn't make a lot of sense when viewed from normal consensus reality. In fact, this was going to be a whole lot of fun. I doubled over with laughter upon hearing this. Her story probably ratcheted the energy of the seminar up several more notches in hilarity as well as in intensity. I told her husband that he might really get worried if she suddenly developed a predilection for listening to hip-hop music!

When you look at someone and your imagination brings up an image of something like a warthog, or a pink feather, or perhaps a pane of glass, ask yourself: "Okay, what does this image mean to me and what should I do with it? How is it helpful in the present moment?" Questions like these are what Tony Robbins calls power questions. By asking them, you get your brain searching for a unique answer. It will also help you to move more readily into a resourceful state, rather than getting stuck in recycling and empowering the images of someone's problem-set.

For instance, if someone tells you that they have a "frozen shoulder" it might be helpful to imagine what would happen if the shoulder was encased in a block of ice that was suddenly exposed to the heat of a noontime summer sun. I have used just such an approach on more than one allegedly "frozen" shoulder.

If you are learning how to draw people, you start by outlining the form with primal shapes: a circle or oval for the head, perhaps a triangle to define areas of the face or jaw, an ovoid or even a rectangle for the torso, and so on. Once you have delineated the basic shapes, you then begin to erase a line here, add a detail there, until you have drawn a fairly accurate and complex rendering of a person. It all starts with establishing the proper perspective, and then you work forward from there until your finished drawing matches something that previously only lived in your imagination.

Everything in nature can be described in terms of geometry. From the dance of atoms to the revolution of the planets, every type of growth and motion is governed by the same sets of laws. These laws are portrayed through the geometric symmetry of shapes and forms. When using these simple geometric shapes in Matrix Energetics, consider for example that the scapula or shoulder blade's basic shape is that of a triangle. The sacrum, which is the bone at the base of the spine, is also essentially triangular in shape.

Now, you have two scapulas: one on the right and another on the left. Imagine that the person you are working with has a high right shoulder, and perhaps even discomfort or pain in that area of the body. One very simple thing to do is to create a wave pattern where all you need to do is adjust the orientation of the involved scapula/triangle. If in your imagination it "looks" too high or tilted, you just re-envision it in the corrected position and the actual bone will move in order to conform more closely to the position you have imagined. It is amazing to watch how a procedure as simple as this can have such a profound and instantly measurable effect.

Using Your Imagination for a Change

Dr. Dunn comments about the role of imagination:

> When I was growing up, my family's prevailing mode of thought was devoted to the concept of rationality. That is the way my grandfather's mind worked, and he passed that quality on to my father, who passed it on to me; and so I was taught the value of rational thought. Imagination did not play a large part in my upbringing; we were taught to see things "as they really are," and there was no other interpretation possible. That was just the way that things were. I was taught that imagination was only for cartoons and that if you wanted something you had to work hard for it!
>
> Richard's imagination is really vivid and magical, and alive with intent, but mine initially was not—it had to be reawakened. So, when Richard said something like, "Imagine an Orca whale swimming in front of you," I couldn't do it. There was nothing there. That is not the reality that you want to play out when contemplating these concepts. If you have tucked your imagination into a little box somewhere, I want you to go and find it and let it out right now. Go and find your imagination box and wherever it is, grab hold of it and put it right in front of your face where you can clearly see it.

Allow it to move forward, unbidden by the dubious contents and constructs of your conscious mind, so that it merges right into the center of your forehead where, like a rose, it opens and springs forth into bloom, bringing into existence new and magical possibilities for your life!

If you haven't taken the time to develop your imagination, maybe you want to start reading comic books, or sci-fi fantasy novels. Entertain new ideas and concepts and do things that you normally wouldn't do, because everything that you think, feel, and do is a potential source of new information. If you really buy in to the quantum model, then everything around you in your world is simply composed of light and information.

One of the early exercises that I gave to my partner in medical practice, Dr. Dunn, was to practice feeling things in such a way that the conscious mind could not track the outcome. If you want to do this, read this description and then close your eyes and imagine yourself sitting with me in my favorite Mexican restaurant, because I know that just like me, you are hungry to learn new things *now*. It is great to do an exercise like this when you are least expecting it because then you don't see it coming in advance, which means that you are caught off guard and can actually learn something in a new way.

So, on that particular day, Dr. Dunn had been working to feel the bones of the skull and to note their differences, and he had been meeting with a lot of frustration. When he told me this I instructed him to close his eyes. I then had him remember the first Star Wars movie where Obi-Wan Kenobi was teaching his young apprentice Luke how to sense the Force.

Surely you remember that scene where the robot droid is floating around his body, engaging Luke's primitive skills with a light saber by firing randomly at him as if they were fencing with lasers. Luke was getting clobbered by the droid, until, at the point of total frustration,

Obi-Wan blindfolds him and has him learn to extend his feelings through the agency of the Force so that he can sense the droid's attack before it actually occurs. At first, Luke gets the worst end of the battle. Then his mind calms and he begins to feel a connection with the movements of the droid. Soon he anticipates and blocks the droid's attack, successfully employing the force to guide his unconscious intuitive responses. This scene, of course, sets the stage for the crucial moment when Luke has to take out the Death Star. Following an intuitive prompting, he disengages his targeting computer, trusting instead his connection with the mystical Force to guide his actions.

When I took Jiu-Jitsu training many years ago, I had to pass a test where I was kneeling blindfolded on a mat, and my sensei was behind me with a wooden sword. The object of the test was to sense the exact moment when the sword blade was about to fall on your head, dealing a potentially fatal blow. At the exact moment of the attack the student must do a forward roll out of harm's way. Imagine the consequences of failing this test in the era when it was undoubtedly conducted at the point of a razor-sharp samurai blade!

Dr. Dunn made his need to learn from me into a struggle, and as one of my wise teachers once commented, "The sense of struggle creates the struggle." The idea here is to let go of what you think you know so that your thoughts can then lead you toward a more desirable new outcome. Remembering Obi-Wan's lesson to Luke, I had Mark close his eyes and imagine that his arms became detached at the elbows. Next, I told him to reattach his elbow joints to the side of his skull just behind the ears.

Further, I instructed him to imagine that his eyeballs floated free of their sockets, coming completely out of his head so that they floated in a 360-degree arc around his head. Satisfied that he had complied fully with my instructions, I told him that he should imagine a hundred skulls floating in a rapid procession before him and that he had one second per head to feel the information that was presented by each one, using his disembodied elbows to touch them in order to elicit the desired information. He proceeded to follow my instructions to the letter. Needless to say, his palpation skills improved immensely after that exercise.

Richard Bandler, one of the founders of Neuro-Linguistic Programming (NLP), did something like this using the principle of sensory overload to improve a client's tennis game. In order to improve his client's serve, Richard blindfolded him and then had several people continuously and mercilessly lob tennis balls at him. As you might imagine, initially this was a very painful and embarrassing incident for the man. Then he managed to return one of the serves, then another, and another. When he finally was allowed to remove the blindfold his game had experienced an exponential leap. He found that he could now often anticipate the serve before it happened.

We blind ourselves all the time to the information that is all around us. One of the easiest ways to become more psychic or intuitive is to simply set the goal in our intent to stop habitually deleting from our conscious attention so much of the information that we process unconsciously.

Healing vs. Transformation

Are we actually healing someone with this work? Who knows! I don't claim to be a healer or to even know what the concept of healing means. The human body is so complex and intricate that we have not even begun to scratch the surface of its mysteries. Look at all of that complexity. Do you think that I, with my very limited knowledge and awareness, know how to heal anything? I don't think so.

This is not to imply that what you might term healing doesn't happen with this work; it happens all the time. I just don't want you to see me as the Doer. That title belongs to God or universal intelligence. What we do, mostly, is to get out of the way. When you do this work, if you can resist the temptation to interpret or make it about something you know, then you can allow it to be about something that you don't know. Or, at least you can be a little unsure, which allows for some wiggle room for that universal element of grace to transform the elements of your life.

A woman came to see me in my office complaining about a number of health challenges. She had rheumatoid arthritis with swan neck deformities on the fingers of both hands. She also had a positive antibody titer for Lyme disease in the past. She suffered from extremely chronic constipation, had pain throughout her body, and insomnia and depression on top of all of that; she was a real mess. During the first three visits, I pulled out all the stops with my clinical knowledge trying to alleviate her symptoms, fix her allergies, and detoxify her body. I employed Homeopathy, drainage remedies, nutrition, and manipulation—everything I could think of—and still at the end of that third office visit she sadly reported that she was no better.

Realizing that what I was doing was not working to any clinically noticeable degree, I opted to try something really different. As I have stated elsewhere, I had the very great honor of training with Lyn Buchanan, one of the original Remote Viewers who worked on the military Stargate project. What I did in this particular instance was not, and I emphasize this point, not Remote Viewing, which requires the careful practice of a rigid scientific protocol. What I did was to assign some random numerical coordinates to symbolically represent my client.

I then allowed the ideo-motor response, similar to dowsing, in my right hand to draw a pattern on paper that I intended to represent the energetic pattern of the woman I was trying to help. In remote viewing this would be *phase one*, where you generate a gestalt image that represents information about the target. What I did was more an intuitive rendering or picture of patterns of energy, which my subconscious represented through what my hand drew on the page.

The first picture was so complex that I didn't see any opening or possibility of change in that pattern. I kept focusing on smaller areas of the initial drawing and then expanding that information on a new sheet of paper using the same initial coordinates. It's kind of like taking a picture of an area with a surveillance satellite, and then focusing in with computer software to enhance and bring out important minute details of the intended target. So, you go from a city block, to a section of road within that block, to focusing on a particular car, and finally enhancing the image enough to read a license plate for the purpose of identifying the owner of the vehicle.

In this same way, I kept drawing on each new sheet of paper patterns that became increasingly refined and simple, until intuitively I drew images on a new page that felt like a resolution rather than merely the more detailed depiction of a problem.

With great excitement, I mentally extracted the liberating pattern of information from the paper, energetically placing the template or essence of it directly into the client's chest or heart chakra using my imagination to affect the transfer. Instantly, she reeled over backward, laughing almost hysterically. "This is new and maybe even encouraging," I thought; "she hasn't done that before." She laughed heartily for at least another ten minutes or so and then appeared to move into a deep trance, remaining absolutely still for the better part of an hour, effectively taking my treatment room hostage to her altered state. That's okay, it's one of the reasons I have more than one room to work in: for just these types of responses.

When I was done practicing for the day I reflected on what had happened. I remembered one of my instructors at Bastyr who taught a course in beginning Ayurvedic medicine. Toward the conclusion of our semester with him, he told us that if we could develop the compassion in our hearts as physicians to such a degree that a person could cry from just our presence in the room, then we were truly on our way to becoming something more, perhaps even healers. Well, this woman had the opposite reaction. What does that imply? Then I remembered a book I'd read whose title asserted that laughter is the best medicine. "We'll see," I muttered to myself.

It was about three weeks later when I saw her again. On the day that she was to return to the office, my secretary looked everywhere for her chart and we just could not find it at all. When she came in for her appointment, I apologized to her and asked if she would mind filling out her patient information again. She responded to me that she couldn't remember why she came in because all of her previous concerns were so much better that she really hadn't given them much thought. When she filled out her new intake form, under chief complaint she wrote "None—I would like more of the same!"

Now, whenever she comes into the office I hold up my hand at chest level in her energy field and she collapses over backward, laughing so heartily that if anyone else is there observing me they get caught up in the spirit of the event and start laughing uncontrollably as well. I have learned from this woman that the spirit of mirth is contagious, and we should all be exposed to it at an early age instead of inoculating ourselves against its effects!

Dr. Dunn comments on this story, concerning why we prefer to engage in methods such as the Two-Point rather than treat symptoms if possible. "You don't want to enter into a problem-set if you can help it; that is why we have this Two-Point process. It can mean anything that you want it to or nothing at all, but most importantly we are not directing energy into a battle with someone's health conditions or their beliefs about healing and disease. If you do a Two-Point, or an Archetype technique, you are not in a big fight with anything."

What you are learning to do within the process of the Two-Point is to create a new game that you can enter into and experience with the power of your active imagination. You want to include a new reality subset of this process working well for you and without effort.

Time Travel and Parallel Realities

As I discussed in the last chapter on Two-Point and Archetypes, you can always begin by using the Two-Point procedure as the starting point for anything you do in Matrix Energetics. This provides you with a simple starting baseline and allows you to always be able to measure your results. The coherent focus of your attention can cause the wave interference patterns of what you have chosen to focus on to disassemble and reorganize into a new pattern. This implies that from a quantum model of altered awareness, you can change the manifestation of a physical outcome simply by coherently looking at it.

The Two-Point procedure allows you to measure what you want to change. Having established your starting point, you then focus your creative will on the pattern. Next, relax and move into an alpha state of relaxation, taking your mind completely off the problem. When your consciousness interacts with the quantum state of matter, the very act of your measured, focused intent causes ripples and undulations of causative action to enfold the observer and the observed together. You have become as one with the object of your intent, momentarily fused together.

I know this sounds as if it should be hard, or perhaps even impossible, but it isn't. Anyone and everyone can do this. Do you remember my story about how I was working on someone's frozen shoulder to no avail? A breakthrough moment came for me when I heard my guides tell me, between their fits of laughter, to "imagine it not there." Sometimes it can be as simple as just that. I know that we all have the ability to do this. Not only is it easier to do than you think, it may even be easier to do than you *can think*. Thinking too much can sometimes get in the way of the desired results. That is why it is better to just "play" at achieving the desired outcome.

After you have practiced regularly applying these ideas for a while, your subconscious mind begins to sift through all of the playful possibilities. Before you know it, you will start to imagine and use many new ways of doing these things with simplicity and elegance. Your approach will be uniquely customized to fit the way your mind works as well as your particular gifts of creative play. You will bring your own unique creativity to this process. If you would like to see confirmation of what I am saying, go to my website and read the stories posted on the message board. It's great to read how somebody else has "made it up, and made it fun!" *What you perceive and endow with the power of your creative intent can become your reality.* With enough practice and conviction you can learn to master the elements of this physical domain. Your world then becomes all about what you make up and decide to live.

Using Questions with Your Two-Point

Questions are one of the means by which you can define and focus states of being. A question such as "What am I noticing now?" prompts the brain to pay attention and retrieve sensory data relevant to the task or target that is the current focus of your awareness. If the questions you find yourself asking are not useful or representative of powerful states, then ask a better question. Try practical questions, such as,

"What would it feel like to collapse the wave now?" Or, "What would this pattern of light and information look like if it were more useful?" Even, "What would have to happen for this to be better now?" Questions like these can create outcomes that are far more useful for yourself and others. At the very least, get in the habit of asking questions that can, and will, engender helpful responses from the universe. You can trust that before you have asked, the answer is there right in front of you. Before you ask, the answer is given.

Time Isn't

Another idea that limits our realities is that healing takes time. And while that may be true for the reality that we inhabit with our senses, our consensual reality, I honestly believe that time is a factor in these things mainly because we have been taught to believe that this is true. The laws of Newtonian physics might loosen up a little in matters of healing and transformation if we just did not give a fig what others thought. Handing the details over to a power greater than yourself is a good idea, because in the so-called spiritual realm the same reality constraints do not apply.

The idea that things happen over time is a misconception or hallucination induced by our brain's temporal software. Even the idea of channeling energy or chi for healing is based on our mistaken belief that healing takes time. *Consider the possibility that in a quantum reality, things can happen instantly.* The events we observe conform to our individual set of expectations and beliefs about how things "really" are. We can experience instantaneous transformation. Our conscious mind, however, with its time-encoded perceptual bias, still experiences events "playing out," or unfolding gradually.

According to relativity theory, time is a variable thing and depends on the perspective of the observer. Have you ever had to spend time with someone whose company you did not particularly enjoy? You might catch yourself in such a situation repeatedly glancing at your watch and wondering when this experience will end. Have you ever noticed how slowly the clock hands appear to advance in such a situation? Contrast this with what it is like with a new lover. You can hardly believe that the few minutes you spent together were actually nine or ten hours. In such instances, your perceptions and internal reference for the passage of time have been altered.

In his book *The Yoga of Time Travel*, Fred Alan Wolf claims, "Through the action of the quantum wave, it is possible for a future event to connect by traveling backward through time, with a present or a past event." One day, while sitting in a restaurant enjoying my well-deserved lunch break, I had a realization concerning this concept. I vividly imagined how photons traveling backward from the future could meet with photons traveling in a forward direction from what we call the past. Where these two waves of photons meet, their point of intersection creates the present moment. The coordinates for our personalized experiences in space/time are formed where the path of these two streams of photons meet.

Fred Alan Wolf says in his book *The Eagle's Quest* that nothing is actually determined as the past. Both the past and the future are connected to the present as possibilities. When you actually do what I have called "The Time Travel Technique" in Matrix Energetics, you begin to discover for yourself that this statement of Dr. Wolf's is not only plausible, but is a highly useful belief to adopt. When you understand what this statement suggests, the concept establishes a solid foundation for you to be able to "move" into your past and reorganize it. You can utilize your skills with the Two-Point method to target the significant time frame for when an injury or another event occurred in your life and access the pattern of waveforms, as well as the emotional and physical "charge" on that event.

The past and the future are really just possible outcomes. They can, to some degree, be altered. You can conceptually entangle the power of your present-time focus with the elements of your past. By allowing for a different, more beneficial outcome as a possibility, a pattern of trauma can resolve right in that instant. The aftermath of this newly configured event can provide a very real basis for physically observable changes.

Or you can even use the idea of parallel worlds, which I will cover in more detail later, to imagine a new outcome in which the event or trauma never occurred in the way you have previously remembered. The really weird part about doing this is that after you have successfully accomplished an activity of this nature, sometimes you or another person involved in your trauma can no longer precisely recall the details of it. In essence, you can learn to Time Travel backward to when something wasn't! Mathematician Roger Penrose presents the logical view that time cannot be pinpointed at all. He wrote, "I suggest that we may actually be going badly wrong when we apply the usual physical rules for time when we consider the (X factor of) consciousness!"

Using Time Travel with Two-Point

The following is one example that illustrates how Time Travel can work in conjunction with Two-Point and intuitively derived archetypes. While demonstrating on a participant in a workshop, I was holding a Two-Point and engaging my active imagination to Time Travel back to a significant time in her life that was related to the process that we were engaged in. I began counting backward and when I mentally reached the age of three, her spine changed right bene' my fingers, while simultaneously I "saw" two archetypal images ir id succession.

The first image was of an old black teapot boili er. Considering this as important information, I asked my inner f ice what I should do with this image. Immediately, I received the that I should turn down the flame on the stove in order to cool e teapot. Following this thought, I "saw" an image of somethi ooked like a fishhook with a worm on it embedded in the w ine at the level of the lower lumbar area. Again, asking me to do, I receive an image that suggested that I needed to str fishhook and release the worm from the hook. So, that is what I did in my imagination. This woman had been experiencing low back pain for a number of years, and she instantly felt better when I addressed these images and released these patterns from within her energy field.

After I told her what I had seen and done with the images, she offered this information to the seminar group, in confirmation of what we had together created and experienced: "When I was three years old, I came down with a very serious case of spinal meningitis and was rushed to the hospital with a temperature of 106 degrees." Now the image of the kettle boiling over made perfect sense. She continued, "While I was in the hospital they did a spinal tap to try to isolate the organism that was causing my fever." And now the image of the bent fishhook embedded in her spine also took on significance! She had told me nothing in terms of any medical history when I began working with her, yet her needs were addressed simply by using the Two-Point, Archetype, and Time Travel techniques.

Steps for Performing Matrix Energetics Time Travel Technique:

1. Perform a measurement as previously taught in the Two-Point Technique.

2. Ask the age of your partner or client. This will become your starting point, or as they called it in the movie *The Philadelphia Experiment*, your Zero Point reference for time.

3. Begin counting backward in five-year increments while holding your Two-Point that you have delineated from the first step.

4. Set your activate so that the quantum waves of change will you wish to "arrive" at the event or time frame that the correct with. You do not have to actually know approximate event, because as you approach the ence, you will begin to feel the two

points that you are holding start to soften and change beneath your hands.

5. Be prepared for the possibility that you or your practice subjects will experience physical or emotional releases of energy when this occurs. Gently support and comfort them, but try not to interfere with or edit their processing of the information and experiences.

6. When things have settled down and reached an apparent conclusion, re-assess with your Two-Point procedure. Repeat the process if necessary, because there may be multiple time frames that need to be accessed to resolve the issue or pattern more completely.

Just as in your practice with the Two-Point procedure, there may be multiple times or events layered into the pattern you are working with. Keep going back to your Time Travel procedure, counting back farther each time until no more change occurs when you do this procedure for the particular event or problem. Take a look at the example of me doing this on the Matrix Energetics website. It is not at all difficult to do. In fact, an orthopedic surgeon corrected a severe scoliosis on a patient just by duplicating what he saw me do on that video clip.

Not only is this technique very simple to do, it is also one of the most useful and productive ideas in the Matrix Energetics bag of tricks. I use this technique constantly in my practice, and it is actually easier to do than it is to describe in print. This is so useful that if you are working on someone's knee, for example, you can imagine traveling back to the time that the knee was injured and change the pattern of the knee injury in the past. This can heal her knee, and may also transform her entire experience of that period in her life, because the two things are related.

Many times we travel back to the moment of somebody's birth process. Often, patterns that can develop into problems of ill health are traceable to events or energies that happened at birth. By reconfiguring the consciousness hologram of the birth process, you can help someone make a new start in life. And obviously, if you can travel back to the moment of birth, you can move even farther into the past. You can calibrate or track patterns that were established anywhere within the journey from conception on, and sometimes even beyond that point.

Consider, as an example, the hypothetical notion that when your mom was about four months pregnant with you, your parents argued a lot. Now, much later in life, perhaps at the age your mother was when she was four months pregnant with you, you suddenly develop acute anxiety for no outwardly apparent reason. I have seen cases where the Time Travel process can instantly resolve problems like this.

Parallel Universes

A corollary to the Time Travel principle is the idea that you can also use this same process to access alternate or parallel realities. Time can be envisioned as a hologram, and the past is configured by the way in which you remember events. But according to quantum theory, at every moment there are multiple possible outcomes. When you begin to change the certainty about how past events are put together, you help re-establish a flexibility of consciousness in which the patterns that hold that event together as a remembered construct can be loosened enough to allow for your mind, that most excellent of Time Travel machines, to *re-encode and enact the sequence of those events differently now.*

Super String theory, the latest candidate for a unifying theory, contends that the universe at its most basic component is composed of vibrating loops of string. In order for the math equations of Super String theory to balance and make sense, it is postulated that our universe must have at the very least eight to twelve dimensions. I don't know if this is true or not, but it is a conceptual reality that can be very useful when doing this work. The idea of parallel dimensions and lives also might be a more scientifically acceptable way to broach the subject of so-called "past lives." I do not know what the truth about reincarnation is, but the idea of past lives can at the very least be a useful fiction that may allow you to resolve chronic patterns of energy that cannot even be approached by any other means. If people are not comfortable with the idea of reincarnation, I call this a Parallel Dimensional Expression, or P.D.E.

Parallel Worlds theory asserts that for any activity there are an infinite number of choices that spring up. The weird part is that scientific proponents of this view of quantum quirkiness say that in order for their mathematical proofs to balance and make sense, for every single possibility out of an infinite array there must spring into existence a parallel world with those specific qualities and features.

Instead of complete worlds arising from every thought and possibility, what if you could move laterally through parallel dimensions with the ability to manifest just one key difference from that other world, and that difference could then be merged and made to out-picture in this one? Cool thought, and also a very imaginative way to problem-solve. In *The Dimensional Structure of Consciousness*, author Samuel Avery speculates wildly that perhaps this is how Jesus fed the multitudes: by multiplying the number of loaves and fishes.

Imagine if Jesus could peer into the other dimensions of possibilities and simply merge with the appropriate world that could provide Him with the requisite number of loaves and fishes. This method is a very useful and playful strategy to consider employing with Matrix Energetics. Am I saying that this is actually possible? Who knows? Is it worth considering as a creative useful fiction? Of course!

What would a therapeutic approach look like using this idea? Very simple. For example, consider the case of someone's chronically painful knee. We find our two points on the structure, which cause them to feel connected, or more stuck, hard, or rigid. Now, perhaps we employ Time Travel, calibrating our temporal destination by feeling/observing a change in the Two-Point pattern, which we are still maintaining with our hands. When we get to the correct time frame we can mentally pose questions and notice whether any of our contemplated courses of action demonstrate a change in our Two–Point contacts.

If we consider the idea of moving laterally across parallel dimensions, and we notice a softening of the tissues underneath our hands, then we "run" with that thought. Now we can get specific; what I would do is to count out loud how many dimensions we would move through. One, two, three, four… and I would feel a change at the fourth level, for example. I then let go of my conscious thoughts, focus my intent, and relax into the quantum wave of transformational change.

If you have followed the steps I have laid out for you, amazing changes can result from this type of approach. I hope that this example, which has very practical applications, helps to pull together and organize some of the previous concepts for you.

Closing Suggestions

Now that you have read this far in the book I have a few practical suggestions for you.

1. Attend a Matrix Energetics seminar with me so that you can really get into the wave of everything that I teach in a group setting.

2. Re-read this book and underline any parts that you have questions about.

3. Read some basic quantum physics books written for the layperson. Check out the bibliography to get some idea where to start.

4. Practice these ideas everywhere, all the time, on everything animate or inanimate.

5. Go to www.matrixenergetics.com and read everything posted on the message board.

6. Watch the support video sections I have posted for people who have purchased this book.

7. Check on my website for any new releases, DVDs, or home study aids that will assist your continued learning process.

8. Believe in yourself and learn to stretch the borders of your imagination.

9. In the words of Yoda, "Either do, or do not. There is no try." Commit to learn all of this stuff no matter how much time and energy it takes to master. It will reap rich dividends in your life.

Nothing that I teach in Matrix Energetics is difficult to do, and it can be readily duplicated by anyone willing to entertain some new ideas and then put them into practice. All of the processes and procedures that we teach are literally so simple and natural that a child could do them. In fact, an eight-year-old boy who took the seminar with his mother can do the things that I have talked about in this book. The science parts in the book may appear a bit complicated to some of you without that kind of academic background, but the concepts are easily understood. Of course, to any scientists who read these same words all I have to say is this:

If you're reading this late at night, my explanations might seem not quite right. And they're not, I just wrote them like that. "It doesn't really matter what chords I play, what words I say, or if my hair is brown. Cause it's only a Northern Song." With a wink and a nod to the Beatles and the late, great George Harrison.

Matrix Energetics encompasses the realms of science and art. Art represents the language of the imagination, while science, to me, is the crystallization of that art into practical laws of manifestation. You can turn your practice of these principles into such reproducible and reliable experiences that for you they can solidify into observable fact.

These tools are now in your hands to use however you may choose; I hope that they serve to enrich your experience of life as much as they have mine.

I am going to touch two points that will allow for a major change in your life. Here is the first one, and there is the second one; they are encoded in my consciousness as I am writing this. Now they are, with your unconscious permission, released into your world as you are reading this. Accept the possibility of this occurring, and move forward into the desired state of change now!

9

The Matrix Seminar Experience

THE SEMINAR EXPERIENCE CREATES A UNIQUE and what can only be described as magical environment where everything is possible and nearly anything goes. Participants shed their preconceptions and limiting concepts and enter a highly supportive playground for the mind. Once the rational left brain realizes that a lot of what is being taught is based on some of the key concepts of quantum physics, some of the so-called "old guard consciousness" can let go of its precarious hold on reality, to be replaced with an often gleeful and frequently outrageous sense of fun.

Participants are often pleasantly perplexed at how their problems seem less demanding and overwhelming after spending a weekend immersed in the pleasant task of creating new solutions to their old and outmoded ways of thinking and being. Not only do you learn to think outside of the box, you begin to suspect that the box doesn't really even exist. When you see your world with new eyes, the way you perceive your life takes on new colorations and hues. Maybe there really is a pot of gold at the end of your own personal rainbow.

Being Playful

Getting deep responses in seconds instead of hours. This is really fabulous stuff! I can tap into the unlimited and not be constrained by the physical world. I learned how to make instant changes in both physical and emotional conditions in a fun and playful way. Feeling the energetic changes, some intensely. Being told that being playful was the key.

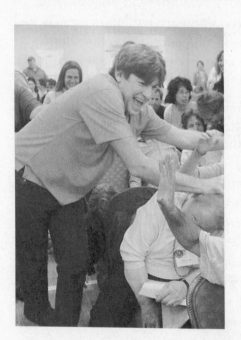

Instantaneous Change

I have not read the Harry Potter books, but from what I gather it seems that J.K. Rowling has set up the next generation to easily get what we have just learned. Validation that I can change my world instantaneously without processing and "therapy-izing." Powerful.

Stretching Reality

The matrix is the frame on which the canvas of reality is stretched, allowing us to move beyond healing and into personal transformation. It is, in fact, a way to reconstruct our reality. Such freedom, so many creative ideas! Hogwarts School of Magic for adults!

Unified Field Theory

I don't need to know anything. All of my past education and paradigms need to be restructured to make use of this experience. Realizing that, I create every facet of my reality through the medium of intention and choice. Matrix Energetics—a unified field theory for all the other things I do and work with.

What a Trip

I have a good imagination and it has been stretched way beyond my comfort zone; I am scrambling to catch up. I know I will get there because I am willing and able—what a trip!

No Limits

Anything you can imagine is possible. Your imagination is the limit.

An Amazing Experience
"I was lying on the floor in front of a hundred people, unable to move my arms and legs while my mind and body were doing God knows what for half an hour. Not only was I okay with that— it was the most wonderful, uncommon, frightening, and amazing experience I have ever had, and the most profound. Thank you."

Opening the Door
The seminar was the miracle. To see what is possible opens the doors to all things in life.

10

Tales from the Matrix

THE FOLLOWING ARE HEALING STORIES about Matrix. I share them with you as examples of the myriad ways in which Matrix Energetics is useful and widely applicable.

Massage or Message?

I'm a massage therapist. I took Matrix Level 1 in June, and Levels 1 and 2 in September. I recently had a client with neck and upper back pain. She said the pain in her C7 neck vertebra was so deep it could not be touched physically. As I "played" with her, her body shifted all her weight to her left side. She then told me that when she was a kid she broke her left leg. After that she had never been able to put her full weight on her left side. She was amazed that all her weight was now on her left side, and she had no pain. I wasn't even aware of, or trying to do anything about, her left leg. It just happened.

Then as I continued, her head tipped way back and she said, "Now that spot in my C7 is being accessed." At that time (in my mind's eye), I saw her as a child in a great deal of fear. I talked to her (in my mind)

161

and asked her if she wanted to let go of the fear. She was too afraid. So I said, "Maybe you could just let go of a cup of it and see how that feels." She did, and she felt okay, so I asked if she'd like to let go of another cup. She did, and then she felt so good that she dumped a whole bucket of fear. *At that very moment*, my client told me the pain in her neck was gone! Then I told her what just happened in my mind, and she said it made perfect sense to her. She left my office with no pain!

—*Darla*

The Crooked Made Straight

I treated a woman who had had back pain for years, almost to the point of being disabled. After one session she felt no pain, and has since been without any pain at all! I used a variety of Matrix Energetics techniques with her. Also, I corrected a scoliosis. I saw two realities side by side, one with scoliosis and one without. I focused on the one without and it worked!

A neck problem of nine months duration disappeared in a minute through Time Travel, to the amazement of the client.

A friend I met during a seminar complained of her long-standing knee problem. I did a Two-Point on each side of the knee, and she said that the knee was beginning to adjust as soon as I bent over to do my Two-Point. Before I touched her! And as soon as I touched the knee, she felt an incredible heat. The whole process took about thirty seconds. Her knee was still pain-free two weeks later.

A man with a recent injury in his arm: I did a non-touch Two-Point on a client's arm from a distance of two feet. I directed one point at his wrist, the other point toward the ceiling. He said that he felt like cold winds were blowing out of his arm, and the pain was gone in one and a half minutes. Regards.

—*Tom*

Wonder of Wonders

I met Richard Bartlett DC, ND, the founder of Matrix Energetics, a few days ago through my friend. I am not surprised by what he does; however, I am so thrilled that science has come to merge with what we have been expecting for a long time. And what is happening is far beyond just quantum physics. I am so happy to become more of who I am.

I have received the power of Matrix Energetics by only attending his talk. After one hour into his talk and demo, my spine aligned by itself, a long-time infection in my right ear was healed, the stiffness in my right shoulder was gone, and I could lift both of my arms up with ease. The next day my body began to detoxify, and I noticed that I could go deeper in my meditation than before the presentation. Love.

—*Mayumi*

The Art of Not Doing

I woke up on Tuesday morning after the Level 1 and 2 Matrix Energetics seminars, wondering just what I had gotten myself into. I felt like my brain was in such overload that I wouldn't be able to remember anything I had learned over the past three days. So I thought that if I couldn't remember, I certainly was not going to be able to use it! That thinking set me up for a perfect lesson in the art of doing nothing.

One of my employees came in that morning feeling like she was at the end of her rope. She was frustrated with a three-year-old daughter who had recently learned how to whine, a husband who wanted his shirts ironed (while she was eating dinner of course), and a couple of clients who were pushing every button she had. All of this was putting her in a pretty cranky state herself.

As she was telling me this story, the thought occurred to me: "If she had a sense of peace about all that was going on with her right now, how would that feel?" I began feeling it in my body, but she just kept talking. As she finished, I asked her if she would like to try some of what we were taught in the seminar and she agreed. As I reached up toward the top of her head, she started to lean forward. Since I wasn't "doing anything" yet, I steadied her and moved around to her side. I put one hand on her head and as my other hand touched her back getting ready to do a Two-Point, she promptly went down to the floor on her butt. It happened so quickly and we were both so surprised that all we could do was laugh. Then she started to cry as her process continued. After a few minutes, she felt completely different: calmer, happier, and ready to take on the day.

This experience was exactly what I needed to get past my own issues of "Can I do this?" It was also a very powerful lesson in how to do absolutely nothing and get awesome, incredible results. So as I played with other people throughout the day, I certainly wasn't worried about the outcome; I was able to trust that it was already done. Matrix Energetics is wonderful. I feel like I have come home.

Two More Mysteries

I used Matrix Energetics on a two-year-old girl. She had been sick for six months, and doctors didn't know what was wrong with her until they found a rare tumor on her spleen a couple of weeks earlier. I did the Two-Point as well as a couple of frequencies, a module, and a few things my guides told me to do. I saw the wave and the changes that were taking place. She got off my massage table and said she felt a lot better. I worked on her on a Monday and she was to go in for another MRI and possible biopsy that Friday. I asked her mother to call me after the MRI and let me know what the doctor had to say. The mother called Friday, crying on the phone, because the doctors couldn't find the tumor. It was gone.

I also worked on a guy who had broken his ankle in two places. They didn't want to do surgery right away because of the swelling. I did the Two-Point technique, a couple of the frequencies, and a module, as well as Time Travel. I watched the wave and could see the bones move back in place. The swelling had gone down when he left. He had a doctor's appointment two days later. They did an MRI on the ankle and it had already started healing. The doctor told him he didn't need to have the surgery after all.

—*Michelle*

The Theory of Relatives

Since the seminar, I've worked on a number of people using what I learned. These are mostly physical issues and the results have been astounding. My sister fell down the stairs about a week ago and was in a lot of pain. I worked with her for a few minutes and she felt 95 percent better. She woke up the next morning feeling right as rain. Boy, did she give me a funny look when she realized she actually felt better. Ha!

It's been almost two weeks since the seminar and I have seen some very definite changes in my life. Not little ones, *big* ones. The first thing I noticed was that my outlook is now very positive. I find it easy to stay relaxed and peaceful. As Richard and Mark would say, I find ways to stay in the solution-set rather than the problem-set. This seems to come quite naturally and is absolutely delightful. This is a big change for me.

I also worked on my ex-wife's arthritis over the phone and got similar results. I'm like a kid with a new toy on Christmas morning. Smile.

I'm simply making space for the best of all possible outcomes and they are happening right before my eyes. I'm seeing synchronicities everywhere and always the solutions are so beautiful to behold. I am awed to witness these things and play a part in them.

Thank you Richard. Thank you Mark. The ideas you both presented, and especially the way you presented them, have made a very big difference in my life. Kindest regards.

—*Grant*

Little Miracles

A child, six years old, punctured his eye with an exacto knife while riding in the car. A couple of weeks later, after ER surgery and medicine, I saw the child. Knowing that we are in the business of transformation, I proceeded to Time Travel, Two-Point, and so on. The grandmother had lost hearing in her left ear due to a car accident. I worked with her too. This was on a Saturday.

That Sunday, the grandmother called me and told me that the little boy complained about the brightness of the light as she changed his clothes in the bedroom. Intrigued, she held up fingers and he could see them. A tremendous improvement for the little guy's eyesight! She also said that now she could hear the dial tone in the phone and if you spoke directly into her ear, she could hear the words. She was excited that she heard a motorcycle pass as she was driving! Matrix never ceases to amaze me! Thank you to all the practitioners and Drs. Bartlett and Dunn.

—*Larry*

Florence's Frozen Shoulder

She came to me with the frozen shoulder title attached to her stiffness. Her physical therapist had worked for months to no avail. Eighteen months earlier, she tripped while hurrying to answer the door and dislocated her left shoulder. She underwent surgery (the scar adhered to the bone) and from then on, she could not raise her arm or lift much at all. She then became so disoriented that her family put her into an assisted living apartment.

Three times we went through Two-Pointing and some frequencies, and each time she could move better at the end of her session, but reverted to the beginning status each week. On visit four, I tried Richard's Time Travel regression and found that her shoulder memory went back seventy-three years! That would make her two and a half years old when it started. So I asked what had happened when she was that age. She looked at me quite oddly and explained that her ring finger had been caught in a slamming door and the tip cut off. They wrapped her finger up very tightly for weeks and little Fannie hugged her hand close to her chest all that time to protect it from further pain. That finger is on the same side as her frozen shoulder.

So we traveled back a little farther, to when Fannie was two years old, and asked for a different response, both physical and emotional, to that injury. After collapsing that wave and adding some soothing frequencies, we tested her range of motion. She had complete movement ability, far better than in the sessions before, and the look in her deep brown eyes was fantastic! She didn't need to come back to see me, and I haven't seen her at the assisted living place. I have, however, been seeing her tooling around town in her big pink Cadillac.

Avoiding Imminent Surgery

In July 2004, two months after my first Matrix seminar, a challenge presented itself. Over many days, my intestinal pain and spasms had increased tremendously, and when my fever suddenly went to 103 degrees, I was admitted to the hospital. They took a CAT scan and diagnosed diverticulitis, along with severe infection. After six days on antibiotics the fever reappeared and my blood pressure shot up. They took another CAT scan, which found the same picture as before. The doctor came to Mike and me and said that since the medicine wasn't working they had to schedule surgery to take out the offending sections of colon. He scheduled a test the next morning to determine which parts to cut out.

This was *not* part of my Reality—cutting my skin! After the initial tears, I knew I had to try Matrix Energetics, even though I felt I had no clue how to do it myself. I called Karijo for help. She told me to go with what came naturally, and she would be supporting from home.

The word "but" carries a lot of emotion, so I asked the question: "What would my intestines be like if they had a different reaction to all the crappy stress, both physical and emotional, from the time of Thanksgiving before I was born to the present?" I Two-Pointed from above my right shoulder diagonally to below the left hip—and *whoa!*

There was a kettledrum, thump-like feeling jolting my body and then thumping the bed. Then I had an unbidden visualization of burnt marshmallow crusts flaking away from my intestines and being gently blown away by the winds. (I had never seen such archetypes before.)

Wow. I could hardly wait to see what might happen in the morning! I called Mike and Karijo to let them know.

After the colonoscopy the next morning, no one was forthcoming with any information. I heard a nurse ask another, "Are you sure these are what came up with 314?" And the reply was, "That's all that came with her."

There was absolutely *no* evidence of the condition they were going to do surgery on. In fact, in the pictures the tissues were very pink, smooth, and healthy. A quite grumpy doctor sent me home the next morning.

Right Time, Right Place, Right Action

Two weeks ago, I sat up in bed, put my feet on the floor to get ready to go to work, sat there for a moment, and decided I wasn't going to work that day. I telephoned in, rolled over, and went back to sleep. An hour later the phone rang. A German lady called and informed me that she and I had talked two years ago, and I told her I could heal her. Me—say that? That's pretty self-assured on my part. Kind of scary, actually. I had no recollection of that conversation or the lady. She went on to explain that she had written my number down and then lost it. She had been searching for two years to try and find my number. Finally, she gave up and the slip of paper fell out of a book that morning. She promptly called me. She again asked me if I could heal her. I simply and humbly replied that I would try. I told her to put the coffee on and I'd be right over.

The doctors had sliced the top of her right foot and cut all the nerve endings. The toes went off to the side and curled under the foot and the big toe went off in the other direction. I did Matrix Energetics and reconnected the nerve endings and brought the toes back into alignment.

I went back in time and found out that when she was a little girl during several lifetimes, she had suffered all types of hurts and traumas. The foot problem was the physical manifestation of those hurts. I was watching a video in my head and as I told her about the scenes I saw, she was right with me and saw the same things. We saw her red tricycle and I told her to put the "fear" in the basket on the front of it. She said she didn't have one. I told her she did now—with red tassels on the handlebars. She asked if she could put her teddy bear in the basket along with the "fear," which she did. She pedaled her tricycle to the bridge, stood up on her tippy toes, and threw the "fear" into the river and watched through the side rails as it floated away. I then reconnected the nerve endings in the foot to the leg.

After the session, she invited me to lunch. As she walked across the room, she stopped in her tracks. She had *no pain* whatsoever. The foot, which was previously curled under, was straight and fully functional. She was in tears. She reports that she continues to improve every day and she is able to stand tall and erect with no pain.

This was at the correct *time*, the correct *place*, and the correct *order*. All I had to do was listen.

—*Jill*

Long Distance

I know someone who has been in multiple car accidents over the last couple of years. She's been in terrible pain. One day, I just did the work for her remotely and then emailed her that I'd done it. She told me that she'd been in so much pain that she couldn't eat. She was returning from a trip and suddenly had no pain while driving. She then called a friend and went to dinner and enjoyed a meal for the first time in days. She returned my email and said she'd felt better at the time I did the work.

—*Maureen*

Balancing Act

I was talking to a friend online. She mentioned that one leg was shorter than the other and her hip hurt. So I asked her to go and look in the mirror and tell me if one hip was higher than the other. Her right one was. So I said, "What would it be like if they were even?" She mentioned that her hips felt funny. I told her to look in the mirror again. Her hips had evened out. The pain was gone.

—*Marie*

The Healing Power of a Mother's Love

I have been healed long distance. I hurt my thumb. The doctors took X-rays and said the thumb was broken and a tendon had been ripped off, and that I would need surgery. I called my mommy (my practitioner) and asked for assistance. She lives in Washington and I live in Colorado. I sat down and over the phone she took me back in time. This time, my thumb went into a bowl of cotton balls instead of the floor. Within the hour my cast was bothersome so I took it off, only to find I had full range of motion and no pain.

When I went to the doctor again they took more X-rays and there was no sign of anything wrong with the thumb. It has not bothered me at all. It also led to me realizing my control issues, changing my perspective on control, and releasing my anger, which raises my positive levels, and so on. Amen for Matrix Energetics.

Rewiring the Brain

I have a friend in Australia who asked me to send Matrix Energetics to his family members in New Zealand. In particular, his brother had suffered with chronic headaches for three years. I "looked" inside his brain and saw that two circuits were crossed over each other. I moved the crossed wires and put the flap back on his head. The next day, my friend informed me his brother's headache had stopped. It's been a month now and he still doesn't have any headaches.

The father had an operation and the doctors couldn't stop the bleeding. My friend asked to intervene, with his father's permission. I did Matrix Energetics from the top of his head to the base of the spinal column. The bleeding stopped the next day. I don't know if I did it or not, but my friend credits me with it.

Matrix Energetics and Animals

I attended the February 2005 Seminar as a small urban farmer who wanted some tools to help out with the day-to-day events of my home. I was a second-time attendee, and wanted to increase my confidence in being effective in applying Matrix Energetics. (Let this be a note to watch out for one's goals!)

The day after the seminar I had my full-time non-farming job to get to, and as usual I was up to feed the "critters" before the sun was up. As I entered the barn, I heard this rather loud, yet occasional bleat. Such a sound makes your hair stand up—it is a sound of newness, of raw life, and simultaneously of shock and pain. It is a sound you should only hear once, not on a sporadic and ongoing basis.

I raced out to the goat pen, and there were two goats standing at right angles with their heads bent to the ground. The ground was muddy and it was cold. I looked for a newborn goat and could see nothing. As I got next to the two goats, I saw a dirty, limp body in the mud. Off to the side in the stall was another body—not moving at all. I picked up the limp newborn and raced to the house. I was scared, and the thought of this marginal life leaving before getting started made me feel helpless. I knew that I should use Matrix Energetics, but I felt frozen with fear. I took the goat to a guest in the house who had also been at the workshop (and was sleeping in bed). She immediately applied a Two-Point and some frequencies, and cuddled up under the blankets with the goat. I went out back and took care of the goat that had passed before I had arrived. When I had finished my chores, I came back in. The goat was alive, has continued to live in good health, and has not had pneumonia or other problems—so very common to young ones who have such starts.

This should have been enough excitement, but there was more to come. A second goat, the young one's grandmother, went into difficult labor three hours later. As I had been reprimanding myself for freezing up for the newborn, I found myself then helping the mother with her labor by Two-Pointing and imagining all working like a greased slope. The baby came out, and then two more! All of them were healthy.

The next day I went out and the sister goat (who was a first-time mother) was kidding—again one baby was dead and the other one could not even cry. I lifted up the baby and could barely feel the heart beating. This time I had nobody to turn to, so I had to apply Matrix Energetics myself. Again, the baby came back and I took her with me to work. We call this goat Mouse because she is so small, and she is alive and doing well, with no disease. For four more days, I had births every day. Once I took care of Mouse, there were no further complications.

I worked twice within a week on a three-year-old Sheltie dog whose owner was going to take her to the veterinarian for a broken rear right ankle and a bump on her hind leg. I saw the owner about a week later and he said his dog did not have to go to the vet, her leg was fine, the small bump was gone, and she had lots of energy and was running around the whole place. I sensed while working on the Sheltie that she was aware of what I was doing. She stood very still both times, although in the first treatment, she occasionally twitched her rear leg. I did both treatments outside in the parking lot of my apartment complex.

I also worked on a horse long distance. He had colic and the vets didn't know what to do because it would keep coming back. I did the Two-Point and Time Travel and a couple of the frequencies, and saw the wave and the change that happened. The owner called to let me know the colic was gone and hasn't come back.

—*Michele*

The Nuts and Bolts of Matrix Energetics

I was hanging around after the seminar and one of the instructors asked me if I would help her change a flat tire. Having changed many tires in my lifetime, I agreed, and we proceeded to get the tools out of the trunk. Now, when I was a kid, lug bolt wrenches were made of heavy steel, and were long—so you could get effective leverage against the tightness of the bolts. Unfortunately, they don't build 'em like they used to. The wrench was short and flimsy. I tried turning the wrench with the strength of my arms to no avail; I stood on it with all of my weight and still nothing. Finally, I jumped up and down on the wrench as hard as I could several times, only to be disappointed. The lug nut would not break loose.

"Here, let me do a Two-Point on it," the instructor said. We both chuckled. As she did the Two-Point, I pressed again on the wrench with my foot and *the bolt came loose with almost no effort!* It was unbelievable. The same thing happened with each of the remaining bolts!

Being one of the world's bigger skeptics, I found this was the kind of solid physical "proof" of the power that is available to us, not only for health issues, but for everyday needs as well. During the seminar, I was sitting too far away to really see the physical results as Dr. Bartlett worked. This experience let me see the power at work in a practical "nuts and bolts" way.

Smooth Sailing

I live on a boat. This year, sadly, I had to take it out of the water for the winter to let it dry out, and moved into accommodations on land. That meant everything had to come off the boat: the boom, the stays, the mast—even screws and shackles and things that have not been budged for five years had to be undone, unscrewed, removed, and stowed. I think both the boat and I were unhappy about this process, to say the least, and things were not going smoothly.

And this is where Matrix Energetics comes in. After a lot of struggle, I tried Two-Pointing, or at any rate, Two-Pointing as I understood it. Every time I encountered a screw or a shackle that was well and truly stuck, I simply Two-Pointed it and "saw" butter or oil running around the threads, making them all shiny and slippery, and each time *on the very next try* the screw or shackle would move as if there had been no difficulty at all in the first place.

The friend who was helping me take the boat apart was amazed, to say the least. Especially when I budged the screw that a big burly mechanic could not get to move with an enormous screwdriver, a wrench, a hammer, and all his might and muscle.

—JKS

Shooting the Wave

I had just picked up a set of sockets from Sears because they had rebates, which made them free (less taxes, of course). I was removing them from their packaging and assembling them on my socket rack when I noticed the smallest socket, which should have been 10mm, was 3/8" instead. 10mm is a very popular size on foreign autos, so I was disappointed, free or not! I took the rack in to show Patty, but it was oriented incorrectly for that purpose. So I attempted to flip it around and ended up dropping it on a large picture frame that was face down across the top of a wastebasket (don't ask why it was there). We both heard the distinctive "tink" of glass fracturing. I reached down and felt underneath with my fingertips and verified that an obvious fracture line was running across the corner that had been assaulted. I gave my apologies and explained what I was trying to show her, even though she wasn't much interested at that point.

As I was leaving the room, I noticed she was "shooting the wave" on the still-prone picture frame, and my immediate (left-brained) thought was "Yeah, right ... good luck with that!" Not more than five minutes later, grinning like the Cheshire cat, she brought me the picture frame. The glass was perfect—no cracks whatsoever!

If I were going to wish for a miracle, I would probably have preferred something on the order of an end to the national deficit. But maybe I'm only ready to accept smaller steps toward the larger miracles right now. Maybe when (or if) I take happenings like this for granted, it will be the larger miracles that tweak my awe. In any case, stuff like this keeps life interesting!

Just observing and grinning inside.

—Mikey

Time Travel

While I was at your seminar, I traveled into the future and left a morning wake-up call for my new/old friend, Angela. The call was to wake her the morning of her birthday and sing "Happy Birthday" to her.

She told me she distinctly remembers having wake-up calls in which all the people she had befriended in her *lifetime* sang "Happy Birthday" to her. Wow! I just set the intention for my voice—she had a chorus of thousands. She said she mentioned this to her parents because it was so uncharacteristic of her to have that happen. Not when we do Matrix Energetics!

Two Points

A couple of points I'd like to mention in case they might be of benefit to others. First, intellectually I needed to make a distinction between setting up the Two-Point, which may involve thinking, feeling, imagining, etc., and "releasing" it, or however you want to describe it (i.e., going to nothing). So it seems to me that there are two steps to the Two-Point, "going to nothing" being one of those. Second, having a sense of trust, combined with an attitude of letting go, was really key for me in getting this to work. By this I mean letting go of the sense that I am doing something to the person, and just trusting deeply/ having faith that whatever needs to happen will happen. It seems to me that *intention* is there as a part of that faith or sense of trust.

So how has it been going? My practice is being continually transformed by Matrix Energetics. I'm getting better results with less effort, and pretty much across the board my patients are experiencing accelerated healing. And all by doing less! It seems that as I surrender my power, my treatments become more powerful.

Frequently Asked Questions

Matrix Energetics: Why that name?

Matrix Energetics refers to the living crystalline energy that constitutes our bodies. Research biologist James Oschman, PhD, describes living systems in this way. Bones, fascia, connective tissue, and even some of the supportive tissues in the brain are composed of a liquid crystalline substance. It is like a crystal in an old radio set. The interesting thing about crystals and crystal structures is that they actually allow for what we call quantum phenomena. There is speculation that a quantum computer that incorporates organic technology and crystals could be built in the near future.

I call this work Matrix Energetics because I don't believe that our physical bodies are the only reality. We basically are light and information—patterns of energy. And that's what topnotch physicists have been saying for the past fifty years. Even if you believe that, it doesn't have much significance in your daily life. *But,* when you learn that you can actually heal someone's conditions, transform his emotional state, or change his mental processes using Matrix Energetics, new possibilities emerge. It is possible to change years-old injury patterns with a light touch and a specific process. Matrix Energetics utilizes the power of focused intent. Matrix Energetics can be learned, and in fact mastered, by anyone.

What's your goal with your work?
My goal with this work is to teach as many people as I can how to have these perceptions and do this, because it's very easy to learn. Mothers can help their children and families can have access to free health care that is right at their own fingertips. Matrix Energetics is a powerful new tool anyone can use to supercharge whatever it is they're already doing to heal and transform, and to do it pretty much instantly.

Can anyone do this work?
Matrix Energetics is available to everyone. In fact, the people who have the most difficulty learning this work are those who have the most college degrees: those who practice a materialistic state of awareness that does not allow for miracles. It's kind of like in *Peter Pan* when Tinker Bell is dying, and you have to believe in fairies to keep Tinker Bell alive. Once you are able to believe in a possibility other than what you have believed or experienced, to entertain that a new idea could be possible, you've entered into that quantum realm where all things are possible.

Is it challenging for most people to enter into a "quantum realm"?
Matrix Energetics is a lot of fun for most people. On the first day of the seminar people begin wondering what's real. By the second day they begin to think, "Well, we're not sure what's real, but we don't care because we're able to do these things that we've never imagined before. This is a lot of fun; let's do it some more." It's necessary to be like a little child and know how to play and how to imagine.

There is a great scene in the movie *Hook*, in which Robin Williams plays the grown-up Peter Pan. He is sitting down with the children, the Lost Boys, and they're playing around the table at having a banquet.

Peter Pan, because he grew up and let his imagination atrophy, is starved because he can't imagine any food. He's getting more and more frustrated. Finally, he starts to play and when he does, the whole table pops into view, filled with a wonderful assortment of food.

It's like that once you start to play with the Matrix Energetics concepts. You begin to accept that your worldview could be big enough to contain ideas that allow for outcomes that appear miraculous. Several quantum physicists I've met are very much like children, in that they are willing to imagine a different reality than everybody else does. They have the mathematics to support their imagination, and they have expanded their belief systems. Yet they can say that this is the way reality must be, because the science and the math confirm that this is the way it must be!

Intent plays a big part in how your work is conducted. Please define intent and describe how it is utilized in your system.
Intent is the energetic foundation for manifesting the substance and structure of your beliefs into observable reality. You've never seen a house built without a blueprint; basically, intent is your blueprint for building that house. If you want to accomplish something, you first have to imagine it. Once you imagine it, then you conceptualize it, you actually see it happening, and then you take steps to actually do it. In Matrix Energetics we have a blueprint called "Science Structure," which we teach in a simple way so that anyone can understand it. It's a lot of fun. Once you understand some really basic principles, you begin to realize that the ideas in quantum physics provide a very real gateway into a realm of possibility that allows for instantaneous healing, physical manifestation, and virtual transformation of every aspect of your life.

Once you understand the basics of Matrix Energetics, you can apply them to the quantum laboratory we call the human body, see the intended changes happen, and decide for yourself if it's real—or not. Once you do that, you have crossed over the border between what you used to believe and what you believe now. And once you do *that*, there is no limit to your imagination and what you can do. This doesn't mean that because you think you can, you should jump out of a building. That's not a good idea; you're trying to override a very powerful consensus reality. Find safe and simple things you can start with that you thought were beyond your capability. I submit to you that you can do many other things that you have only dreamed about.

What do you perceive matter, physical reality, to be?
Matter exists because we have thought it into existence and because there are so many of us holding the persistent delusion or reality that there is such a thing. We've made it up so well that we've made it physical. We have taken background cosmic energy and transformed it with our awareness and consciousness into our experience of what we call our reality. But our reality is really what we create inside of our minds. Wayne Dyer talks about this in his new book, *The Power of Intention*. He combines elements of quantum physics with Carlos Castaneda, a famous writer, philosopher, and teacher who presented the teachings of Yaqui Indian shaman don Juan in his books.

Don Juan teaches that we need to learn to *See*, not just look at things. He made the distinction that when you look at something, you're looking at it through your perceptual filters; you're seeing what you are taught to see, what you've been accustomed to seeing. When you actually See something, you look beyond the veil and start to apprehend or become aware of the energy patterns that make up that existence. Now, this is not to say that in order to do this work you have to be able to do that—you don't have to be clairvoyant. It is important that you embrace the concept that we all are energy and we're really composed of this quantum stuff from which we co-create our objective experience of reality.

Does someone have to "believe" for Matrix Energetics to work?
I have a cat story that speaks to this. I think cats only have two beliefs: They should be fed and they should be master of the household. One

day, a kitten came into my office with a broken foreleg that had not set properly—it was having trouble walking on it. The kitten had never met me, had never heard about Matrix Energetics, and did not have expectations. I picked it up, held two points, one above the break and one below the break, touching lightly for about thirty seconds. Then I heard this snap; the bone reset and the kitten was just purring and perfectly happy. Half an hour later, when I came out of my office from working with another client, it was jumping off furniture with absolutely no problems. This animal didn't have any belief, not even an unconscious belief in what I do. It is not necessary to have a preset notion that this will work, only to observe and be able to validate what happened in your experience. You can believe me when I say that the changes that occur are usually obvious, often dramatic, and easily observable by anyone.

Explain what you mean about Time Travel.

Well, it's funny because you could say we're making it all up, and one of my mentors, Dr. Richard Bandler, says that's okay—if it's a useful fiction. It may not be true, but if it's a good enough belief system that it works consistently, I'll take it. I mean this very literally. I can touch someone's body, feel tension there or pain or whatever you want to look for, travel backward in time conceptually, and feel the change in tissue under my hands when I get to the point where the injury actually occurred or the condition began. That doesn't mean I believe that I can heal cancer or any disease. I don't believe in healing and I don't believe in disease. I believe in transformation, because healing and disease are two sides of the same coin.

Why do you prefer to use the word "transformation" instead of "healing"?

Healing is a nebulous concept; what it means to you might be completely different from what it means to me. Healing is also a very abstract term, just as disease is an abstract concept. To a scientist or a medical doctor, disease describes a set of symptoms, signs, clinical findings, and laboratory tests that tells her or him that this collection of symptoms has been named to be this disorder. Just naming something to be this disorder, and having this collection of symptoms, in no way defines what the person has. We are not talking about the disease that has the person; we are talking about the person who has the disease. That's why I say I don't believe in disease. Take Fibromyalgia, for example. What does it mean? It means that there's pain in the connective tissue and muscles—so what! That's not a disease, it's a description. Same thing with techniques or therapeutics; most therapeutics are tools that are designed to address a certain component of functional or pathological disorders. They are just someone's thought/belief designed to address the components of the condition they are observing and attempting to "cure."

You're taking a concept of healing to address a concept of disease: You can call it treatment, you can call it therapy, and I prefer to call it gone. That's not to say I'm so arrogant as to believe that will always be the case, but wouldn't it be nice to believe that? Isn't it better to believe that you can transform in an instant rather than think that healing has to take time? Or, that without pain there is no gain—that's one I just love.

At the quantum level there are infinite amounts of energy in a very, very small amount of time. The energy cannot be observed, so we don't know what it is. Physicist Richard Feynman said that perhaps the subquantum world contains morality, or composers, or giraffes, or whatnot; he didn't really know. I think that's where miracles happen, where all the possibilities come together. When you apply a miraculous sense or non-consensus reality approach to something that's been construed to be a very physical condition, a conflict arises. You run headlong into consensus reality; you run into codified beliefs about what disease or healing is.

Where does the transformation take place?

I believe it has to be at the energetic level where mind and matter meet, and are essentially the same. We're talking about photons—light—and information, and that's about all there is. I have to believe that transformation takes place at the submolecular level, the quantum level. That's where you get the effects of infinite energy and infinitesimally small amounts of time. Richard Feynman said you could have potentially anything occur in an infinitesimally small amount of time.

How does quantum physics fit into the work of Matrix Energetics?

There's something called the Heisenberg Uncertainty Principle. It essentially says that you cannot observe a system without entering into that observation and therefore changing it. Scientifically, this means that if you look at something and attempt to measure its velocity, you lose track of its actual location. If you try to track its location, you lose the ability to measure its velocity. You can never actually measure both at the same time; you can observe one and change the other. I started to realize that our consciousness is functioning at this quantum level to create our reality all the time. The reality we get is what we accept, what we've been taught to believe.

There are things such as spontaneous remission. Miracles fall outside of the realm of linear physics, but quantum physics actually predicts miracles. We now have quantum physicists who are calling this unified field theory the Mind of God. Gregg Braden has talked about this in depth. If you are dealing with the mind of God, and you're actually a functional part of that mind, you have access to that same awareness.

What do you mean when you talk about filters?

Our conscious expectation of what is or is not possible is formulated by the nature and extent of our beliefs. Our beliefs function as the perceptual filter that dictates what we are able to notice and to interact with as our concrete, observable reality. We call this consensus reality.

Everybody agrees, for instance, that if somebody is wearing a red shirt, the shirt is red. But from a physics perspective, it isn't red; it's every other color but red. Red is the one color that's not there, so it's the one that's being reflected back to us! That's a basic example of how our perceptions can trick us. They can be totally off base, yet be accepted by everyone as real.

I've seen some people fall to the ground when being worked on. Does that have to happen for Matrix Energetics to work?
People experience what seem and feel like very subtle shifts in their bodies. Often these shifts have deep-reaching aspects, and just as often are subtle. Either way, a transformation takes place. Something happens each and every time; that is the beauty and ease of this system. There are more subtle shifts at times, and often people suddenly relax deeply into a slump, and then sit back up renewed and feeling quite different. There does not have to be any dramatic collapsing for this shift to take place and to produce change.

BIBLIOGRAPHY

Atwater, F. Holmes. *Captain of My Ship, Master of My Soul: Living with Guidance*. Charlottesville, VA: Hampton Roads Publishing, 2001.

Avery, Samuel. *The Dimensional Structure of Consciousness: A Physical Basis for Immaterialism*. Lexington, KY: Compari, 1995.

Bandler, Richard. *Using Your Brain for a Change*. Moab, UT: Real People, 1985.

Barbour, Julian. *The End of Time: The Next Revolution in Physics*. New York: Oxford University Press, 1999.

Braden, Gregg. *The Isaiah Effect: Decoding the Lost Science of Prayer and Prophecy*. New York: Harmony Books, 2000.

DeMarco, Frank. *Muddy Tracks: Exploring an Unexpected Reality*. Charlottesville, VA: Hampton Roads Publishing, 2001.

Dyer, Wayne W. *The Power of Intention: Learning to Co-create Your World Your Way*. Carlsbad, CA: Hay House, 2004.

Ellyard, Lawrence. *The Reiki Guide*. Winchester, U.K.: O-Books, 2006.

Fox, Matthew, and Rupert Sheldrake. *The Physics of Angels: Exploring the Realm Where Science and Spirit Meet*. San Francisco: HarperSanFrancisco, 1996.

Friedman, Norman. *The Hidden Domain: Home of the Quantum Wave Function, Nature's Creative Source*. Eugene, OR: The Woodbridge Group, 1997.

Gleick, James. *Isaac Newton*. New York: Random House, 2003.

Gott III, J. Richard. *Time Travel in Einstein's Universe: The Physical Possibilities of Travel Through Time*. Boston: Houghton Mifflin, 2001.

Kaufman, Steven. *Unified Reality Theory: The Evolution of Existence into Experience*. Milwaukee, WI: Destiny Toad Press, 2002.

Kraft, Dean. *A Touch of Hope: A Hands-On Healer Shares the Miraculous Power of Touch*. New York: Berkley Publishing Group, 1999.

Laszlo, Ervin. *Science and the Akashic Field: An Integral Theory of Everything*. Rochester, VT: Inner Traditions, 2004.

————. *Science and the Reenchantment of the Cosmos: The Rise of the Integral Vision of Reality*. Rochester, VT: Inner Traditions, 2006.

McMoneagle, Joseph W. *Mind Trek: Exploring Consciousness, Time, and Space Through Remote Viewing.* Charlottesville, VA: Hampton Roads Publishing, 1993.

———. *Remote Viewing Secrets: A Handbook.* Charlottesville, VA: Hampton Roads Publishing, 2000.

McTaggart, Lynne. *The Field: The Quest for the Secret Force of the Universe.* London: HarperCollins, 2001.

Mindell, Arnold, PhD. *Quantum Mind: The Edge Between Physics and Psychology.* Portland, OR: Lao Tse Press, 2000.

Oschman, James. *Energy Medicine in Therapeutics and Human Performance.* Burlington, MA: Butterworth-Heinemann, 2003.

———. *Energy Medicine: The Scientific Basis.* Edinburgh: Churchill Livingstone, 2000.

Talbot, Michael. *The Holographic Universe.* New York: HarperCollins, 1991.

Tiller, William A., PhD. *Science and Human Transformation: Subtle Energies, Intentionality, and Consciousness.* Walnut Creek, CA: Pavior Publishing, 1997.

Tiller, William A., PhD, Walter E. Dibble Jr., PhD, and Michael J. Kohane, PhD. *Conscious Acts of Creation: The Emergence of a New Physics.* Walnut Creek, CA: Pavior Publishing, 1997.

Walker, Evan Harris. *The Physics of Consciousness: The Quantum Mind and the Meaning of Life.* Cambridge, MA: Perseus Books, 2000.

Whitmont, Edward, MD. *The Alchemy of Healing: Psyche and Soma.* Berkeley, CA: North Atlantic Books, 1993.

Wolf, Fred Alan. *The Eagle's Quest: A Physicist's Search for Truth in the Heart of the Shamanic World.* New York: Simon & Schuster, 1991.

———. *Parallel Universes: The Search for Other Worlds.* New York: Simon & Schuster, 1988.

———. *Yoga of Time Travel: How the Mind Can Defeat Time.* Wheaton, IL: Theosophical Publishing House, 2004.